1675

Swift Arrow

by
Josephine Cunnington Edwards

TEACH Services, Inc.
www.TEACHServices.com

PRINTED IN
THE UNITED STATES OF AMERICA

Copyright © 2007 TEACH Services, Inc.
ISBN-13: 978-1-57258-080-0 (Paperback)
ISBN-13: 978-1-57258-986-5 (eBook)
Library of Congress Control Number: 97-60096

Published by
TEACH Services, Inc.
www.TEACHServices.com

Table of Contents

Introduction

On Tower Hill in the great city of London, William Penn was born and went to school. William, son of an English admiral, grew up among the religious people called Quakers. When he reached manhood, he became a leader of the Quakers.

These Quakers differed from most Englishmen because they did not follow the Catholic religion of the king. Rather, they worshiped God in their own way. Through the years, many Quakers were sent to prison or even put to death because of their religion. By 1680 this persecution had grown so bad that William Penn decided his people should seek a new home in the faraway land of America.

It happened that William's father had once lent King Charles II £16,000. When William's father died, the king had not yet paid the debt. Now William asked Charles to pay by giving him some land in America. The king agreed, granting William over forty-thousand square miles in an eastern area of America that had thick forests.

William suggested that this territory be called "Sylvania," the Latin word for woods. The king added "Penn" in honor of William's father, so the land became known as Pennsylvania, or "Penn's Woods."

Many Quakers found new freedom in Pennsylvania. Within two years the village of Philadelphia had grown to a country town containing 2,500 people. William declared he wanted a garden planted around every house of this town of "brotherly love." At the same time, other settlers spread into the forest, building homes there.

Thousands of Indians lived in these forests. The Indian braves hunted deer, bears, wolves, foxes, and many other animals among the trees, using their flesh for meat and their skins for clothing and wigwams. Their women planted corn and other vegetables to stew with the meat. The Indians lived differently from the settlers, and some Quakers thought them wild and savage. On the other hand, the Indians felt suspicious of these strange people who were moving in, taking over much of the good hunting grounds.

William Penn wanted to keep peace with the Indians. At a place called Shakamaxon, just north of Philadelphia, he met with the Indians, paid them for their land, and made a peace treaty. He explained that Quakers were peace-loving people who believed in justice and goodwill to all men. The Indians promised to live in love with William Penn and his children as long as grass shall grow, and rivers run, and the sun and moon endure. There is no record of this treaty of love ever being broken as long as William lived. Among the early settlers in the new colony were many from the German states along the Rhine. Mennonites, who left their homeland because of persecution, settled near Philadelphia in an area that became known as Germantown. A little later many Lutherans from the Palatinate came and established settlements such as Eaton, Allentown, Reading, and Lebanon.

In all these places they hewed down trees, built sturdy log houses, planted flax between the stumps of forest, and began their new life. These people were the first to introduce the spinning and weaving of linen cloth in America. They spun fine linen thread on small spinning wheels run by foot treadles. They also started the first paper mill in America and were the first to print an edition of the Bible in a European language.

*The big linchpinned wagons rolled forward
and the Boylans, with fourteen other families,
headed West toward the thick forests.*

Chapter 1

Adventure In Their Blood

George Boylan looked up from the spelling word he had copied on his slate and listened to the two voices coming from the parlor. Pa and Grandpa Boylan must be at it again, he thought.

His eyes grew serious as their voices became louder and louder. Every once in a while Pa's voice rose even louder and more excited than Grandpa's. And he could guess what they were arguing about—the same thing that Pa had been speaking of all winter long.

"Well, so long as they're arguing, I hope Pa wins."

With that thought he grinned, pushed his chair back from the table, and crept down the hall as close to the parlor doorway as he dared go without being seen.

"Marcus, I just don't understand," Grandpa was saying. "You have your wife, your family, a big sturdy house, and a fine piece of land here. We're never troubled with Indians, we have a smithy to shoe our horses, a sawmill to cut the timber, and a gristmill to grind our flour. Why, we've even got a doctor now. Why do you want to leave all this for a place where you'll find nothing but trees, wild animals, and Indians?"

"Father, you've just answered your own question. It's so—so tame here. No adventure! We've got everything we need except adventure. You of all people should understand. First you moved from the Palatinate in the Old World to Massachusetts. Then you took Mother and us children from there to New York. And finally you

1

moved here to Pennsylvania. Well, I want to strike out for myself now. And so do a lot of the other fellows. It's in our blood; we've got to go!"

Grandpa considered a few seconds before answering. "Well, Son, if you don't think of yourself, then think of your family. You'll have to yank George out of school and make the children live rough lives always in fear of a raid from those savages out there."

"Now, George is no problem," Pa said. "He's seven years old and so big and strong you could take him for a couple years older. Already he can do a lot of man's work. And if Zella and the baby grow up like him, they'll be no problem either."

Hearing this made George's chest swell big.

"I'd best remember to mend that harness tomorrow like Pa asked me to do," he thought, "or else Pa might change his mind about me being able to do a man's work."

"But what about the children's schooling, Marcus?" Ma's soft, gentle voice asked. George had not realized she was in there.

"Why, you can teach them, Prudence! You can read and write and do sums just as good as any man. What other school do they need? And some hard work will be good for those young 'uns too. I helped Father chop the trees that made his cabin. Now George will help me with the trees for my cabin." Since nobody said anything else, Pa continued.

"No, my mind's made up. We're leaving as soon as the thaw is through and the ground hardens up. There's just too much good, rich land going to waste back in them forests. I aim to claim some of it for my own." When Pa talked like that, George knew he meant business. He felt so excited he could hold it in no longer.

"Whoopee!" he yelled, and ran laughing into the front room. "I can't wait, Pa! I can't wait to start chopping them trees!"

Pa looked up surprised.

"George Boylan, were you sneaking around that corner listening to us?" Pa said it quietly, but his hard, steady eyes seemed to bore holes through George. Now George felt ashamed for listening.

"Get up to bed before I give you a good licking," Pa said. "I don't want my children sneaking around where they have no business being!"

George's head dropped, but he obeyed Pa and without another word climbed upstairs to bed. He felt bad that he had caused Pa to scold him. His curiosity had gotten the best of him. But he couldn't feel bad for long. He was too happy about the move his family would soon make—west into the forests. George could hardly sleep that night for excitement.

The next morning when George came downstairs for breakfast, it seemed that Pa had also forgotten about last night's scolding.

Pa sat at the table, waiting for breakfast. "Prudence, you're going to be surprised at the beauty of the land back there. I hear tell that the forests in the valleys stretch as far as you can see, high mountains rise against the skyline, and streams rush down from them mountains to water the land."

"Your father and his friends were just as excited about this country when they came here," Ma reminded him, setting steaming hot corn bread on the table.

"You're right," Pa answered. "And this land was just fine for them when they came here. The land was rich, and they enjoyed their freedom to worship as they pleased. But now it's different. The area has become too crowded. When our sons have grown up there won't even be enough land to divide among them."

Then Pa turned to George. "Well, Son, how long you figure it'll take you to pack?"

3

"I could get all packed today, Pa."

"Listen to the boy!" Ma broke in. "I'm afraid it's going to take the rest of us longer than that, George. So if you'll be ready so soon, you can just help us."

As the days passed, George found that Ma was right. They were busier than he had imagined possible. First Pa called a meeting of the other young men of the town to see which ones would join them. It turned out that fourteen other families decided to go.

Now the Boylan family began the big job of deciding what to take with them and what to leave. Pa explained they could take nothing but absolute necessities because they would have only one wagon to haul their supplies in. While George's younger sister, Zella, helped Ma sort their clothes, dishes, and furniture, George helped Pa sort the tools and store enough food to last them for the trip and through the next winter. Grandpa Boylan helped them, too, and George was surprised at how much he knew about pioneering. He knew from past experience just which tools they should take and which ones they could make after they reached the new country. And he knew about how much food they would need. It seemed to George that most all the wagon would be filled with food supplies.

The days slipped into weeks and the ground turned harder every day under the bright spring sunshine. One day Pa announced that they would be ready to leave in one week. Now even Ma seemed excited. She flew around the house making last-minute preparations and talked gaily to her friends of the move ahead of them.

George helped Pa put the finishing touches on the big linch-pinned wagon they had made to carry the family and supplies. Then they stretched coarse white cloth across the tall, curved wooden ribs that covered the wagon. Pa selected the best of their cows, pigs, chickens, and sheep. They would take these with them and give the rest to Grandpa Boylan. At last the long-awaited night came when George went to bed knowing it was his last time to sleep in this familiar house. The next morning they were leaving.

Chapter 2

Building a House from Logs

George turned to take one last look at the neat log house he had lived in for all his seven years. It seemed strange to see the door barred in the daytime, no curtains at the windows, and no chickens in the side yard. Then he turned around and swung up next to Pa on the high wooden seat of their wagon. George noticed that Pa didn't even look back. He yelled excitedly to the oxen pulling their wagon.

"Yah! Yah! Get along there. Yah!"

Clouds of dust rose from the road as the big wagons slowly rolled forward. Men shouted at their oxen, and the other animals set up a frightful noise as they moved along beside the wagons. It seemed that all the animals were bellowing at once—cows mooing, pigs snorting, and sheep bleating. Pa jumped to the ground to urge his livestock on.

George heard Ma inside the wagon calling good-bye to Grandpa and Grandma Boylan. Then Grandpa was walking alongside Pa. George waved good-bye, and Pa stretched out his strong, firm hand to clasp Grandpa's wrinkled one. Tears glistened in Grandpa's eyes.

"Don't forget, Marcus, there's danger in them woods," Grandpa shouted above the noise. "Be careful of the Indians. Few of the ones as far back as you're going have ever heard of William Penn or his treaty of love. Don't let George wander from your sight."

Pa grinned. "Don't worry, Pa. I'll teach George to take care of himself and the Indians too."

And with that the Boylan family, along with fourteen other families, were off on their adventure. George didn't know whether or not Grandpa was right about the Indians, but he didn't really care. He wasn't afraid—not even of redskins!

Traveling slowly into the forest, sometimes cutting their own roads as they went and moving only four or five miles a day, these pioneers could not know that the disagreements between England and America had finally reached a head, resulting in the American Revolutionary War. Soon after they left Germantown, Paul Revere, an engraver and silversmith in Massachusetts, went on his famous ride, warning the farmers of the invading English redcoats. The battles of Lexington and Concord were fought, but young George Boylan and his family heard nothing of them. They just continued to urge their oxen over the strange ground, eager to reach their new home.

As night approached they drew their wagons into a meadow or glade and allowed their livestock to graze. Then George would run with the other boys his age to gather sticks and brush for the huge bonfire the men built. They needed this fire not only for light, heat, and cooking, but to scare off the wild animals that prowled close by.

When the boys saw that the fire was blazing and they had carried enough water from some nearby spring or river for their mothers, they would gather at the edge of the clearing or else explore the edge of the woods for small animals or unusual insects. Sometimes they found little harmless green snakes that they hid in their pockets and saved until later in the evening when everyone had gathered around the campfire. Then they would pull out the snakes and watch all the girls scream. It worked every time! Always with George when they played was George's best friend, Robert Stewart. Robert was skinnier and weaker than any of the other boys, but George enjoyed looking out for him. And though he might tease Robert once in a while or playfully wrestle him to the ground, he made sure none of the other boys did anything to hurt his friend.

On the eleventh day out, the wagon train pulled to a halt at the top of a hill. The most beautiful country these settlers had ever seen stretched around them.

Jumping down from his wagon, Marcus Boylan threw up his hands and called, "This is it, folks! This is what we've been looking for. Have you ever seen such beautiful, rich land?"

George caught his father's excitement. To the west and the north rose high wooded mountains; flowers, tall grass, and wide shade trees carpeted the valley below.

"Look, Pa," George called softly. "There to the right, see the fawn?" A little fawn was curiously poking his head around a tree to see what these strangers wanted. A mother deer soon came up behind him. She stood looking but a moment, and then they both disappeared silently into the woods.

"Sure, Son," Pa said. "These woods must be filled with all sorts of wild critters. And take a look at them streams running down into the valley. They'll give us all the water we need and fish to spare."

The settlers climbed back into their wagons and began the slow descent to their new valley home. Marcus Boylan staked out a large piece of ground for his family's land. This section had many trees that would need to be cut, but the land was rich for farming.

That night the settlers met around a campfire to plan the work ahead of them. They decided to live in the wagons until their homes were built. They would build the cabins one at a time, all pitching in to help. The Boylan and Stewart cabins would be the first built, since these families had the youngest children.

George had never been so excited. Every time he had a minute to spare, he ran to the woods for his favorite game—exploring. He discovered new kinds of trees, plants, and flowers and some animals he'd never seen before. But every time he returned to the settlement, he noticed a worried look on his mother's face.

"George, I don't want you going off in them woods without your father," she finally said one day. "We don't know what all's back there yet, and it's certainly no place for a boy to be playing."

"Aw, Ma," George protested, "I don't go far. And anyway, there's nothing back there to hurt me."

But even Pa insisted that George stay away from the woods. "Your ma's right, Boy. What we don't know about them woods is how many Indians live in them and whether they're friendly or not. So you'd best stay close to me for a while, leastways until I can teach you something about the woods and getting along with redskins."

With everybody helping, the Boylan cabin went up fast. Marcus had laid out careful plans for a large cabin, and he even built a lean-to on the back for extra storage. George and his friends worked too, mixing mud and pushing it into the chinks between the logs so cold air and snow could not blow in during the winter.

At night, after the other workers had gone home, Pa would split logs in half, and spend long hours making them smooth. These were to be used for the floor of the cabin. This was another job George could help do. He had an adz like Pa's, except George's was smaller. An adz looked like an ax with the head turned sideways, but it had a thinner, more curved blade for smoothing wood. Most nights the Stewarts came over, and Mr. Stewart and little Robert joined in with their adzes. It seemed to George that Robert was getting weaker all the time. He had grown thinner until his hands looked as thin and delicate as a girl's, and he had a worried look in his eyes.

"Something bothering you, Robert?" George asked one night.

"Well, nothing much." Robert hesitated. "But I can't help being scared of the Indians out there. I hear tell they even scalp people."

9

Mrs. Stewart came over to where the boys worked. "Robert Stewart, are you talking about them Indians again?" she asked. "I don't want to hear you talking about them anymore. You get yourself too worked up."

"Sure, Boy," Mr. Stewart looked up from his work. "The Indians aren't anything to be scared of. Probably aren't any for miles around."

Then George saw Mr. Stewart wink at Pa, but he noticed that Pa didn't return the wink. He just shook his head and went back to work.

Next morning the Boylans rode down to the Stewarts' property to begin work on their cabin. The Stewarts were to be their nearest neighbors. Within a few minutes the other wagons arrived, filled with people ready to work. By noon they had the land cleared and some of the men had already started to cut the logs for the cabin. Pa called George aside.

"Son, I didn't like the way Stewart was talking so lightly about the Indians last night. Truth of the matter is, there's probably a couple of them watching us all the time to see what we plan to do. They don't like people tearing up their hunting grounds. And like your Grandpa Boylan said, they've probably never heard of William Penn's treaty around here." "You mean they really are something to be afraid of, Pa?" George asked. "Like Robert said?"

"Well, no, you don't have to be afraid of them." Pa spoke slowly, seeming to choose his words carefully. "You just have to be careful of them. Practice walking quietly in the woods like the Indians do. Don't step on sticks when you can help it, and step lightly and quickly. If you should see an Indian, don't cry out or run. Just take cover quickly behind a bush or some trees. And there's something else I want to tell you. Your life could depend on it, so listen carefully. If you should ever run afoul of the Indians, don't act scared. Do you hear me? Never, never show fear."

"Pa, that might be hard to do. I'd probably be terribly afraid."

Pa looked at George sternly. "Practice control, Boy. Just practice." Then Pa turned and walked away.

Within a few months the pioneers had finished all the cabins and settled down to their new lives. George spent part of every day helping Pa tend the potatoes, corn, and other vegetables they had planted soon after arriving. Evenings they spent fixing up the inside of the cabin. They made a smooth wooden dining table and even put up some shelves for the dishes Ma had brought with her. Sometimes Ma said they worked too hard.

"No, Prudence," Pa would answer. "I took you away from a nice, comfortable home. And if God gives me the strength, I will have you a neat, good home on the frontier too."

George was hacking at some tough branches with all his might when suddenly the head of his hatchet flew off and hit his head.

Chapter 3

At Home on the Frontier

No matter how busy Pa was, he took time every night after supper to read several chapters from the big family Bible. He read them out loud while the whole family listened.

One night Pa had just begun to read when he suddenly stopped. "Why, Marcus, is something wrong?" Ma asked.

"Prudence, move away from that window," Pa said. "I thought I heard something outside."

By this time George was standing on tiptoe looking out the peephole in their door. "What do you see out there, Son?" Pa asked.

"Pa, there's two Indians walking down the front path, just as plain as you please. What do you suppose they want?"

"Don't know, Son, but I reckon we'll soon find out. Prudence, take the children away from the door." Then Pa unbarred the door and threw it open. George felt scared enough to cry but remembered what Pa had said about not showing fear.

The two Indians stopped at the doorway and raised their right hands in greeting. Then they rubbed their hands over their stomachs. "Many days, no food," one of them said with difficulty.

Pa smiled. "Say, Prudence, these fellows seem to be trying to say they're hungry. How about rustling them up some food?"

Then the Indians came inside and stood looking around at the strange house. This gave George a good chance to look them over. Their skin was darker than his, and they had long black hair and dark eyes. What clothes they wore were made from animal skins, and they didn't look too clean. He noticed in particular that they didn't smile at all.

"Maybe they're nervous too," he thought, and had to smile himself at the idea that these wild-looking people might be nervous.

After that, Indians stopped by the houses of the various settlers every few days, and the women always fixed them some food. Now the settlers were more careful than ever to be on their guard. At first George thought the appearance of these friendly Indians meant they didn't have to worry anymore. When he mentioned this to his father, Pa shook his head.

"No, George, we still have reason to be careful, because now we know for sure that Indians live around here. There are whole tribes that believe that the settlers have cheated them out of their land, and they are determined to get it back and get revenge too."

"Then there's another thing to consider. Remember those soldiers who passed through here a few weeks ago? They told us there's a war going on between England and the colonies. It seems the Indians are using it to take advantage of the colonists."

Then when Pa saw a concerned look cloud George's face, he ruffled George's hair and said, "Don't look so worried, Boy. Remember even though we live with danger, there's good Indians as well as bad ones. Yes, remember that."

As an extra precaution, Pa never went any distance from the house without taking the whole family along. Soon all the families were doing the same.

One morning when George was busy splitting kindling, Pa called him to get in the wagon and go with the family to the Stewarts.

"Aw, Pa, I'm just in the middle of this. Why don't the rest of you go on and let me finish?"

Pa walked over and pulled him sharply by the arm. "George, you don't seem to understand. Did I ever tell you about what happened in Deerfield?"

"Deerfield? Ain't that a town up in Massachusetts?" George asked as he climbed onto the wagon seat.

"That's right. It was an outpost that had trouble with Indians. Finally the Indians attacked the place, killing a lot of the people, and stealing a boy about your age. He was lucky because he found his way back. We don't want any Indians stealing you, George. That's why we take you with us."

George just grinned. "What would Indians want with me? I'm too little."

"Well, we're just not taking any chances," Pa said.

They soon came in sight of the Stewart clearing, and Robert ran out to meet them.

"Say, Pa," George said. "I hope the Indians never get hold of Robert. I think that being away from his mother would kill him."

"If the Indians didn't kill him first," Pa said, shaking his head. "Indians don't think much of crybabies. I'm afraid Mrs. Stewart is not even getting that boy ready for life in a peaceful frontier settlement, much less for some emergency that might come up."

George and Robert spent the day helping their fathers dig stumps out of some ground that Mr. Stewart wanted to plant the next spring. George enjoyed the work and made a game of trying to keep up with the men. But Robert got tired quickly and stopped often to rest.

The next morning the Stewarts came to the Boylans' house to clear trees from some land that Pa wanted to plant next spring. That was the day George had an unusual accident that he was to be happy for, years later. He was hacking away at some tough branches with all his might, when suddenly the head of his hatchet flew off and

15

came down and dug into the top of his head. George felt a sharp, fiery sting as the blade hit him. Then all went black.

When he awoke a few minutes later, the whole forest seemed to be swimming around him. Pa bent over, holding something to the back of George's head. Pa's face looked as white as snow.

"How you feel, Son?"

"My head is whirling, Pa. Everything's going round in circles." "Well, you'll be all right as soon as we get you back to the cabin." Pa and Mr. Stewart made a saddle of their hands and carried George to the house. Ma washed the wound and put a tight bandage across it. Then George spent almost two weeks lying on his mother and father's big, plump feather bed. Whenever he tried to get up, the room started whirling again, but he felt ashamed to lie in bed while everybody else worked. Mother kept the deep cut wet with arnica so it would not fester, and the arnica always stung like bees and ants when she put it on him.

Finally the day came when Ma said he could get up and walk around, and before long he was working again like normal. A long, jagged scar formed over the place where the cut had been. George was glad his thick hair covered it up.

By the time the weather turned cold that fall, the settlers had all stored away plenty of vegetables that they harvested from their early spring plantings. They stored them in root holes dug in the ground. The fruit trees they had planted still looked like leafy buggy whips, but the settlers had no trouble finding crabapples, wild plums, and huckleberries in the forest. Pa robbed a bee tree of enough honey to give a crock full to every family.

Ma made George and Zella study their reading and writing, and she helped them work arithmetic problems on the slates they had brought with them. The family spent the evenings around the fireplace, popping corn and cracking nuts.

George enjoyed the winter, but he was anxious for spring to come. Pa was just as eager. He talked all winter of the piece of land at the top of the hill which he wanted to clear for spring planting.

"It's level and the ground is as black as my boot," he declared, looking restlessly out the window at the snow-covered fields. "I declare, it's April and still snowing. I've never seen the cold hang on so long."

"Oh, yes, you have," Ma said, laughing. "You are just restless, Marcus." "I'm restless too," George said, flexing his muscles proudly. "I want to do some work myself."

"Well, I'll admit you sure have grown this winter," Pa said. "Look at all the new clothes your Ma had to make to replace the ones you've outgrown. You're going to be a big help to me this year, even bigger than last year I reckon."

The days grew gradually warmer, and the early spring sunshine melted the snow. Finally the day arrived when the Stewart family drew up their wagon outside the Boylan cabin, ready to help Pa with spring plowing. George felt so happy that he wanted to run all around the house and shout, but he settled for just running outside and hollering "Whoopee! Come on Robert, I'll race you to the big oak tree!" As usual George finished the race far ahead of Robert, but Robert didn't seem to mind. George noticed that Robert looked thinner than ever and decided he must have been sick most of the winter.

When they got back to the cabin, Ma made them sit down with the rest and drink a cup of hot sassafras tea with honey.

Mrs. Stewart was delighted to sit at the long, smooth table and sip her tea. "I do declare," she said, "I do like to get away from my own four walls for a change. How nice your cabin looks, Prudence!"

Ma smiled brightly. She had a knack for fixing things, and her work-worn hands had done much to make the big room look homey and comfortable.

"I have good helpers," she said modestly, nodding to Pa and George. "The men are always tinkering around here on rainy days. They even pegged me those shelves there this winter."

Neat shelves, with smaller pegs underneath, lined each side of the fireplace. Ladles, dippers, kettles, and big iron spoons hung from the pegs. A butter mold, tin candlesticks, a lantern of punched tin, a butter paddle, and several pretty dishes were arranged on two of the shelves. A third shelf held an expensive clock which Ma was particularly proud of. The fourth shelf held the family library—the big Bible, a battered copy of Pilgrim's Progress, a faded speller, and several reading and arithmetic books.

By now Pa and Mr. Stewart were anxious to get to the plowing. They got up to leave. "You boys wait awhile before coming up so that when you come you can bring us some cool water," Pa told George. "Fill your water buckets at that spring halfway up the hill. Bring your hatchets, too, so you can help us some."

After the men left for the new field, George did some chores for his mother. First he dipped water for her from the spring behind the house. Then he carried in a stack of firewood and rebuilt the fire in the fireplace. Finally he caught a chicken that she wanted to roast for dinner. By the time George and Robert started out for the field, it was almost ten o'clock.

As the boys walked along swinging water buckets, George thought he had never seen a more beautiful spring day. Rays of sunlight filtered through the trees, early spring flowers nodded in the breeze, and the leaves whispered in the treetops. It seemed that every bird in the forest was singing, and, except for Pa's repeated warnings about controlling his feelings, George would have sung with them.

Looking back on that day, George could never figure how one that had begun so beautifully could end so horribly.

A dozen Indians, red and white designs painted on their faces and yelling weird sounds, swarmed through the house and yard.

Chapter 4

Stolen by Indians

George and Robert felt hot and thirsty by the time they reached the spring halfway up the hill. George threw himself on the ground by the spring and gulped the cool, clear water. Robert dipped some water with his cupped hand and drank too. Then they filled their buckets with water for their fathers and continued on their way.

The path wound around through the brush, following a rail fence George had helped Pa build to keep animals out of the fields. Like a true pioneer's son, George walked quietly, watching the ground for rattlesnakes and the bushes for any signs of danger. But Robert didn't seem to care. He tramped ahead, kicking sticks and making so much noise that he alarmed George.

"Robert," George said, "hasn't your pa taught you to walk quietly? If any Indians are around, they're sure to hear you coming."

"Indians?" Robert's high voice squeaked. "My pa told me there ain't no danger from Indians anymore. There ain't no need to be careful at all."

"But there is danger, Robert. Pa says we can learn from the Indians to walk as quiet as a shadow in the grass. There'll be danger aplenty so long as this war continues and the English tell the Indians to—."

"I won't listen about the war and the Injuns," Robert said. "It scares me, and Mamma says it's bad for me to be scared. It makes me shiver and get sick, it does. Now, George, you quit scaring me!"

George looked at his pale, shivering friend, and just shook his head. Robert's blue eyes were round with fright. In order to calm him,

21

George walked ahead a few steps, parted the branches of a big bush, and pointed to a cardinal's nest. He had moved the branches so quietly that the little mother bird did not start or fly away. She chirped once and continued to sit on her nest of eggs.

"See, Robert?" George whispered. "She knows I won't hurt her." He brought the branches together again softly. The boys continued their hike, and George noticed that Robert walked a little quieter now.

They came to the edge of the clearing and saw their fathers off in the distance, working like tiny toy men against a bright blue sky. They had hitched a team of oxen to a big stump, and the great beasts were pulling with all their strength while the men pried from behind the stump with long iron-tipped pikes.

Then George's alert eyes caught a movement in the bushes to the left of the clearing. It had been a swift movement, hardly noticeable, and could have been just a small animal. But George had learned not to take chances. He walked a few more steps, but the movement in the bush did not happen again. Now he felt sure that something besides an animal hid behind that bush. An animal would have continued to move. George was too far from Pa to call him, and Pa had taught him not to run when he suspected danger. So he decided to hide.

George caught hold of Robert's arm and pulled him back into the bushes. He tried to show Robert how to hide.

"What's the matter with you, George?"

"I saw a strange movement in them bushes to the right, Robert. It might be Indians, so sit here and be still while I try to cover our tracks."

"Indians? No, George, don't go. Don't leave me. The Indians will scalp me for sure."

Robert began to cry and thrash at the bushes with his arms. Then he started to wail long, loud cries. Now George really did feel scared.

"Hush, Robert, hush. If they hear us, we won't stand a chance." But Robert cried even louder.

"Please, Robert, be quiet. If Indians are out there, they're sure to hear you. Be quiet."

Robert stopped crying now, but he began to make loud hiccuping sounds. He was trying hard to obey George.

The next thing George knew, Robert gave out a loud scream, and a dark hand pulled the boy out of the bush. Then a hand clamped over George's mouth, and he was roughly pulled through the bush too.

George tried to take a bite out of the hand that held him, but the Indian was too fast. He pulled his hand away, and tied a strong leather strap across George's mouth before George could make a sound. George felt so scared he could hardly move. But Robert was thrashing and kicking, trying to wriggle away from the strong hands that held him. The Indian that had taken George let him go and pointed to the path ahead, meaning that George should follow it. George started walking. He saw no sense in trying to run from these big men who could take care of him with just one arrow. But as soon as the Indian let Robert go, the boy tried to run to the bushes. The Indian just picked him up lightly and carried the struggling boy under his arm.

"You catch a brave. I catch a papoose," remarked the Indian who carried Robert.

The Indian set Robert down again, and again he tried to run. But this time his legs gave out and he fell down. George thought Robert's legs looked like Ma's boiled noodles. Now the Indian got angry. He shouted at Robert and hit him on the side of his head. The other Indian poked the tip of his bow against George's back, steering him through the woods.

George tried to remember what Pa had said. Don't cry. Don't scream. Act brave, even if you're scared. George had never been more scared in his life. But following Pa's advice seemed to have helped him this far, so he knew he must continue to follow it.

"I wish they'd take this dirty strap from my mouth," George thought. "Then I could tell Robert to be quiet and stop running. Besides, it tastes terrible."

But Robert was beyond help by now. He hung limply under the Indian's arm, no longer squirming, but sighing and moaning. Then they came near the clearing where the Boylan cabin stood. George heard his old dog Shep howl. It was the strange howl that he used only when he sensed the Indians were hiding nearby. Whenever the Boylans heard that howl, they would hurry out the back door of their cabin and slip through the garden to a strip of woods by a low cliff. There Pa had dug a cellar for them to hide in. George hoped Ma had gotten Zella, the baby, Mrs. Stewart, and her daughter Becky into the cellar. He didn't know what the Indians would do next.

They rounded a bend in the path, and the Boylan cabin stood in full view. George watched amazed as at least a dozen Indians, red and white designs painted on their faces and yelling weird sounds, swarmed through the cabin and the yard. Then the Indians seemed to be dragging all the furniture out of the house—fat white feather beds, bright quilts that Ma had worked so hard to make, the clock, pots and kettles, and more things than George could take in at one glance. Feathers from the pillows and mattresses flew around the yard like snowflakes. George caught a last glance of gray smoke billowing from one of the cabin windows.

Staggering along the path, with his house now out of sight and the Indian's bow still poking into his back, George wondered how it was possible that flowers still bloomed along the path and birds sang as if nothing terrible had happened. Was it only half an hour ago that the day had seemed so bright and pretty?

After what George guessed was another half an hour, the boys and their captors reached a clearing deep in the woods where about twenty more Indians were gathered. George realized that this was the Indian camp. If only Pa had known about it. Now the Indians untied the straps that had gagged the boys' mouths, but tied their hands and feet. The Indians left the boys lying at the edge of the clearing and joined the other Indians. Robert wailed loudly.

"Be quiet," George said. "Please be quiet. Your crying's just going to get us in more trouble. Besides, our pas will probably come rescue us before nighttime."

But Robert didn't seem to hear. He just kept crying, and the Indians who were now huddled together seemed to be making some decision. They looked up often to glare angrily at Robert. It seemed to George that the Indians were talking all at once.

"They must be discussing what to do with us." The thought made him shiver. What if Pa didn't find them?

Finally the Indians left their huddle and one came over and untied the boys. He grabbed them each by an arm and led them to a pony, lifting them to its back. The Indian tied the boys to the pony and then tied the reins of the pony to his own pony. The red and white designs painted on the warrior's face scared Robert so badly that he started crying again. The other Indians mounted their ponies and rode single file into the dark forest, the one warrior leading Robert and George behind.

They had not ridden far when Robert's steady crying began to annoy even George. "Please be brave, Robert. Don't waste your strength crying. You may need it later if we get a chance to escape."

"I can't help it, George. I just can't. And these straps hurt my legs so bad."

George looked down at Robert's legs and saw that the leather

25

straps that tied them had cut into the flesh of his ankles, making them swell and bleed. He felt sure the Indians would loosen the straps if they saw how they cut Robert's legs. Come to think of it, they were cutting his own legs too. He tried to guide their pony closer to the warrior who led them. "Hey, you!" he shouted. "Hey! Look at his legs." And when the Indian turned around to look, George pointed to Robert's bruised ankles. Surely the Indians would take pity.

The warrior only laughed. He called to the warrior in front of him, pointing to Robert's legs, and the second Indian laughed too. But George wouldn't give up so easily. He kept shouting and pointing to Robert's legs. Finally the Indian at the head of the line called a halt. Then he turned his pony and came back to see what George was shouting about. George recognized him as the same Indian who had first captured him. He pointed to his friend's ankles, now turned a purplish color. The Indian hardly glanced at Robert's legs. Instead, he grabbed hold of the straps that tied George's legs and began to loosen them.

"No!" George cried. "Not mine. His!" He reached to take the straps from the Indian's hands, but the Indian had already untied them. Then another warrior, tall and stern, came back to the boys and loosened the straps on Robert's legs. But he didn't untie them completely.

Now the boys rode more comfortably. Robert settled down to a quiet, steady whine and slumped against the ropes that tied him to the pony.

"Good thing they tied him," George thought. "Otherwise he'd fall off." It seemed that they had ridden for hours, but the Indians showed no sign of stopping. Each time his pony's feet struck the path, George knew they had gone another foot from home. By now they must be miles away. How could Pa possibly find him?

George wondered if Ma and Pa were even alive. And had the Indians completely burned their cabin? His stomach started making little growling noises, and he realized it was empty. He hadn't eaten since early morning. Then he couldn't help thinking of the dinner Ma had been cooking when he and Robert left the cabin. She had already set the beans to bubbling in the iron pot that hung over the fireplace. He had caught that chicken for her to roast, and when they had chicken she always mixed flour and eggs and grease and buttermilk together for drop dumplings. Ma said she planned to have a dish of green onions and lettuce fresh from the garden, their first salad since last summer. The tender little lettuce leaves would have been no bigger than a kitten's ears.

The Indian in front of George was munching on a stick of something hard and black. Then George noticed that all the Indians down the line were eating things they pulled from their packs. But none of them thought to give food to the boys.

The sun dipped into the west, leaving blood-red streaks of color in the sky, but the Indians still kept moving. The woods looked blue in the twilight, and a chill settled in the air. "No wonder Pa told me to learn to endure," George thought. "There's no end to what these redskins will endure."

Darkness fell, and about an hour later the travelers rode into a lovely glade. Bright moonlight lit it almost as light as day. A stream gurgled somewhere close-by. Here the Indians stopped for the night. When a tall Indian lifted Robert to the ground, the boy's legs crumpled under him and he lay motionless. Then the Indian lifted George down. George tried to walk, but he had taken no more than a few steps when his legs gave out too. "My legs feel like strands of cobweb," he thought.

George lay still awhile; then he whispered to Robert. "I hear a brook somewhere close. Let's go get a drink." Robert looked at him but didn't say a word. He seemed not to recognize George. George found the brook himself. After drinking, he dipped some water onto a large curved stone for Robert. But Robert wouldn't drink.

Then George lay still again, listening to the sounds of the forest and the Indians preparing their camp. With every crackling sound in the trees and every distant noise, George expected Pa to come and pull him back into the forest. But help didn't come.

At last an Indian came over with a piece of dried venison for each of the boys. The deer meat was black, dry and dirty, but George was so hungry it almost tasted good. Robert ate only part of his meat, then let it drop to the ground.

"You eat mine, George," he whispered. "It makes me sick."

By the time George finished the second piece, an Indian brought them a blanket. "Sleep," he said and then walked away.

George drew up close to Robert and pulled the blanket over them. In a few minutes Robert's even breathing told George his friend was asleep. George could not remember ever feeling sadder. He continued to listen to the sounds of the woods. What could be keeping Pa? Then a few minutes later George slept too.

Chapter 5

A Strange Tug-of-War

George awoke to the cheerful sounds of the early morning forest. Birds sang, small animals rattled the underbrush, and leaves rustled in the tops of the tall trees. But he didn't feel very cheerful himself. Tears clouded his eyes as he watched the Indians tie loads to their shaggy ponies. Others fixed breakfast over a fire. He knew that in a few minutes they would be on their way again, going farther and farther from his home settlement. It seemed now that Pa couldn't possibly find him. Then he heard Robert stir, and he quickly dried his eyes with the back of his hands. Robert must not see him cry.

"You awake, Robert?" George tried to sound cheerful, but Robert only moaned. George turned and saw that his friend looked wild-eyed and was crying softly. Could this be the same boy who had started gaily up the hill with him only yesterday? Robert's cries came louder and louder. Hearing this, two Indians came near, waving their tomahawks. They shouted fiercely at Robert, who only cried louder. George's heart stood still. Would these savages kill Robert right before his eyes?

"Robert, sit up and be quiet," George said softly. "Then they'll leave you alone." George's calmness seemed to help Robert, for he sat up then and tried to stop crying. The Indians brought each of them corn mixed with venison. It tasted good to George, but again Robert ate only a few mouthfuls.

The same Indian who had led their pony the day before now appeared and led them to the area where the ponies were tethered, bundles already packed on their backs. The Indian lifted Robert onto a pony's back, and tied him on tightly. He seemed to take special pleasure in yanking hard at the straps around Robert's ankles. Blood oozed out from under the straps.

George's face turned red, and he thought fast. Quickly he tore two pockets from his buckskin coat. Shoving them into the Indian's hand, he pointed to the cruel straps.

"Put them under the straps," he said excitedly. "Put them under." George doubted that the Indian could understand his words, yet he seemed to understand the meaning. He slowly untied Robert's straps and retied them, putting the pockets between the straps and the bruised ankles. Like yesterday, the Indian tied the pony to his own.

Then, much to George's surprise, he called for another pony. A young Indian brave brought up a sleek brown and white pony, and the older Indian motioned for George to climb on. The brave placed the reins in George's hands, and the two Indians walked away.

"Why, they're not even going to tie me today," George thought. "They're going to let me guide my own pony. I guess Pa's advice was good after all. It pays to act brave even when you're scared almost to death." At that thought George even managed a grin.

After a few days on the trail George picked up a few words of the Indian language. Whenever he tried using them, the Indians looked surprised but pleased. Remembering Pa's advice, he kept a careful watch on everything and began to learn the Indian customs. He discovered that the more he cooperated with the Indians the better they treated him.

One morning the Indian warrior who watched after the boys waved his arm to catch George's attention and beckoned for George to follow him. George had just awakened and still felt sleepy-eyed, but he obediently followed. What could the big warrior want now? Was he taking George to the forest to get rid of him there? George followed the Indian to a large clearing where the Indian ponies roamed. Then the Indian swept his arm toward the ponies. "Come. We get ponies," he said.

George sighed with relief. The Indian only wanted George to help him round up the ponies. What fun he had now with the Indian, racing after the ponies and leading them back to camp. For the first time in days George really felt like laughing, and he and the Indian laughed together. When they had caught all the ponies, George was out of breath, but the Indian didn't seem tired at all. He strode quickly to camp, and George had to run to keep up with him. Once at camp, another Indian brought George his breakfast, a serving twice as big as they had ever given him before.

"Maybe these Indians aren't so bad after all," George thought as he hungrily slurped up his breakfast. "So long as I'm going to be with them, I may as well enjoy it as much as possible—at least until I can escape." And that was George's biggest ambition to escape to some settlement or town and get some men to help rescue Robert. Then he and Robert would find their way home. He hoped that if he cooperated with the Indians they would give him enough freedom that he could make a run for it when the chance came.

Now George purposely watched for chances to help his captors. Every morning, after helping his warrior friend round up the ponies, he would help load them with the Indians' bundles. George wondered what was in them. At night he helped unload the bundles. George even tried his hand at fixing Indian stew—carefully scraping corn from the cobs and cutting hard venison into small chunks to mix with the corn. He pulled up some small wild onions that he found in the forest and mixed them in the stew too. The Indians smacked their lips with pleasure.

George also hoped that by cooperating he could make up for the way Robert acted. For Robert certainly didn't cooperate. He remained tearful and silent. He seemed to know only that the Indians took him farther and farther from home. When they told him to do something, he just drooped his head and stood still. When they untied his cords at night, he immediately fell to the ground. The Indians had to tie Robert to his pony while they rode to keep him from falling off. And every day they seemed to become more displeased with him, treating him roughly and shouting fierce commands that he paid no attention to.

After about three weeks of hard, steady riding from sunup until long after sundown, the little party reached a large Indian camp situated behind a high hill. Many wigwams crowded together on the grassy plain. George guessed there must be more than a hundred of them. The Indians made their wigwams from animal hides stretched over poles. They had a rounded top, and a big flap served as a door. As George watched, dozens of squaws and children poured out of the wigwams to greet the returning party. And almost as many dogs woke up from late afternoon naps to run after the horses and bark their greeting.

George and Robert seemed to have been forgotten in the excitement. But not for long. Once the warriors had greeted their families again, the boys discovered that they were the center of attention, the most valuable prize of the raid. Old squaws reached out hands to touch their pale skin, little children stared curiously, and dogs growled suspiciously. George had never felt more uncomfortable. But he didn't know how to avoid their stares, because he and Robert had not been given a place to go.

After walking around the camp for about an hour, George caught sight of his warrior friend, whose name he had discovered was Woonsak, coming toward him. Behind him came Robert, looking wide-eyed and fearful as usual.

"You come with me," Woonsak said in his own language, and George understood.

"He wants us to follow him," George told Robert.

They followed Woonsak to a wigwam on the edge of a clearing at the center of the camp.

"My home. You stay here with squaw and papoose." Woonsak again spoke in his own language.

"He says we are to live here with his family, Robert," George explained. Sometimes George surprised himself at how quickly he was learning to understand the strange Indian words.

After the first few days, the Indians paid little attention to the two paleface boys. George helped Woonsak when he could, but most often Woonsak hunted animals for food with the other braves. George spent most of his time walking quietly through the village, wishing with all his heart to escape.

Often he would hunt up Robert and try to cheer him. He almost always could find Robert sitting in the shade by the side of Woonsak's wigwam. "Look, Robert. I brought you a dish of stew one of the squaws gave me." Robert had lost much weight, and George worried that he'd starve to death.

"I don't want it, George. I'm not hungry."

"Not hungry? Why, you haven't eaten all day, and you hardly ate yesterday."

"I can't eat that dirty food, George. It tastes awful. I don't know how you can eat it."

"It's not so good as my ma's cooking, but still it ain't too bad. In fact, I sort of like it. Come on, try a little. You've got to get strong so we can run hard when we get the chance to escape.

Robert pushed George's hand away and began to sob. "I don't want it!" "Well, then, how about taking a walk around the camp with

33

me? There's a stream on the other side with cool water. Maybe you'll feel hungrier when we get back."

"I'm too tired, George. Please, just let me be." And Robert lay down again in the shade of the wigwam. George just shook his head and walked away. He'd go to the stream by himself.

One night, about a week after they had settled in the big camp, George was awakened by the noise of many voices and hoarse Indian laughter. George had gone to sleep that night, and now as he crept silently to the wigwam, he saw many Indian men gathered at the center of the camp. One sat so close George could almost reach out and touch him. In a few minutes all the laughing stopped, and the Indians began what George thought must be a serious powpow.

George listened closely to what they said, but he couldn't make out more than a few words. They talked too fast for him to understand. After about half an hour of talking, several of the braves left and soon returned dragging large bundles that looked like the ones George had helped tie on the ponies so often before reaching camp.

Then one tall Indian slowly stood up, and carefully emptied a bundle on the ground. What George saw made his heart sink. Tumbled on the ground were ornaments and household tools that could have come only from settlers' homes.

"This must be what they took from my settlement," George thought. "That's what I so carefully tied on the ponies!"

Now the Indians emptied more of the bundles, and George caught sight of many things he recognized as his mother's—her blue stoneware pitcher from which he had often poured cold buttermilk, copper kettles, her shell-trimmed handkerchief box, a red garnet brooch, and piles and piles of the blankets, quilts, and linens she had worked so hard to make. George wanted to scream out in despair, but he didn't dare. He just sat tensely in the shadows, choking back big sobs.

Before George had time to do anything more, a sturdy old Indian, his skin brown and dried by the sun, quickly jumped up and barked a short command. George recognized him as the Indian leader. Immediately braves began separating the stolen goods into two heaps. They laid his mother's blankets and linens in a third heap. Then the old Indian took a long stick, walked to the edge of the clearing, and started back drawing a line on the ground through the center of the circle of Indians, through to a smaller center clearing, which the Indians sat around, and on through the other side of the circle of Indians. The Indians were now divided down the center, half on one side of the line and half on the other, with a line through the empty center clearing.

The old Indian returned to the center and pointed to two strong braves, one from each side, and they came forward. The old Indian tied their right hands together with buckskin thongs, and the braves stepped to the center line, one on each side. Now each began pulling in his own direction with all his strength. George realized that they were trying to pull each other over the line. Something like a tug-of-war, he thought.

George leaned forward, eager to see the outcome. Shadows from the flickering fire danced on the dark, muscular bodies of the struggling braves. Back and forth they moved, tugging and straining, heavy corded muscles rippling in their backs and arms. George decided the old Indian had chosen the braves wisely. They seemed evenly matched. Suddenly the Indian on the left stretched out his foot, kicking the other from behind. The surprised Indian fell slightly forward, then regained his balance and suddenly jerked backwards. Now he stretched out his leg, too, as if to kick, but quickly brought it back, giving another sudden jerk in his direction. His opponent started forward and it seemed as if the other might win. The watching Indians, until now silent, cheered and screamed, calling encouragement to one or the other brave. After just a few minutes, the braves slowed down, seeming to be tired. Then with a last mighty burst of strength, one Indian dragged the other across the line. It was all over. The brave on the left had won, and the other Indians cheered loudly. The defeated Indian retook his place in the crowd while the winner stood tall in the center clearing, his face unmoved but his arms folded proudly across his broad, heaving chest.

George felt a surge of dislike for this tall, proud Indian. Whatever he had won, George suspected it belonged to Ma.

Then the old Indian stepped forward again and held up his hand for silence. He pointed to a brave from the side whose warrior had lost the tug-of-war and said a few words. The brave immediately walked to the pile of Ma's blankets and dumped them onto the pile of house-wares heaped on the winner's side.

"So that's what the tug-of-war was about," George thought. "It was a contest to see which side would win the blankets."

Now the Indians were dividing the stolen goods among themselves. George thought he would cry when he saw one Indian holding Ma's fine clock and curiously turning the hands around and around.

"Ain't that your ma's clock?" a voice whispered behind George. George jumped. It was Robert. He had thought Robert was asleep.

"How long you been watching?" George asked.

"All the cheering woke me up. But I feel sick. I mean really sick. I guess I'll go back to sleep." George noticed that Robert could hardly walk.

George continued to watch the Indians and was surprised to see that none of them seemed dissatisfied over the results of the contest. Instead, they all sat down again and began a weird chant with words that George had never heard before. A brave carried a big drum to the center of the circle and began beating it in a steady rhythm. The drum had been made from a hollow section of a log with a buckskin stretched tightly across it. George had seen this drum before, and he knew the drumsticks were made of buckskin too. They were filled with hair and fastened to sticks. George guessed the sticks to be about eight inches long. Now three more braves took their places around the drum, and they also began beating it. The chanting came louder and faster.

Still sitting in the shadows of the wigwam's door flap, George watched with open mouth. He couldn't help thinking of the happy times he had spent with his family singing songs around the fireplace, some songs of the New World and many songs his grandparents had brought from Germany.

All at once, as if by some given signal, several warriors jumped into the middle of the circle and began a strange dance. Up and down they bent, all the while turning in circles, leaping into the air, and setting up a loud, monotonous howl. Soon several more braves jumped into the circle, then more and more, until dancing braves filled the whole clearing, their wild, leaping forms making tall, flickering shadows in the firelight.

After many minutes of watching, George decided he had seen enough and returned to his blanket to sleep. But the dancing figures seemed to leap at him in the darkness. Not in all the weeks since he had been stolen from home had he felt so unhappy. The howling, chanting voices outside the wigwam kept reminding him that never could he enjoy this strange, savage life, never could he accept it. Somehow he must find his way home—if not this month then next month, if not this year, then some other year. He didn't know when he'd get his chance; he only felt certain it would come.

On a hill to the right, George saw the Indian scout. The scout sat quietly on his pony, watching him with an expressionless face. George pretended not to see him and rode a little farther ahead.

Chapter 6

"Act Brave, Robert!"

George stretched in his blanket and opened his eyes. Morning light filled the wigwam. Then he remembered the wild Indian dance the night before, and he sat up quickly. Loud talking came to him from outside, and he poked his head out the wigwam flap, half expecting to see the Indians still gathered in a circle. But the circle was clear. Instead, Indians hustled busily all around the camp.

"I must have overslept," he thought. Usually George went to bed early and was one of the first to wake up. But last night had been different. It seemed that he tossed on the dirt floor for hours while the Indians danced and chanted. The noise had slowly lessened as individual Indians must have wandered off, and not until then had George slept.

Looking out the flap, George saw that some of the Indians busied themselves with unusual activity. Squaws stuffed dried venison and vegetables into sacks that their braves tied onto ponies. Other Indians piled blankets and bundles of equipment on the ponies. George guessed that they were preparing to leave camp, and he noticed that most of these braves were the same ones who had traveled with him and Robert from home.

George turned to roll up his blanket and saw that Robert's eyes were open. "Get up, Robert. I think we're leaving camp today. Most of the Indians we traveled with before are packing their ponies."

Tears streamed down Robert's thin cheeks. "Oh, I can't, George. I'm too sick. My head aches and my eyes burn. I wish Ma was here!"

"Why, sure you do. I wish my ma was here too. But she ain't, and there's nothing I can do about it—not yet, at least." Then George laid his hand on Robert's forehead and felt the hot skin.

"I guess you really are sick, Robert. But you'll still have to get up. If only you'd eat, you'd probably get better."

Then George left the wigwam and ran across the clearing to the field where the Indians kept their ponies. If he was going to be traveling, he might as well get his pony ready. When he reached the edge of camp where the braves were packing their ponies, he saw that Robert's pony was already blanketed and ready. That's funny, he thought, but continued running toward the field.

Just then a strong hand grabbed his arm and brought him to a sharp halt. Turning around, he was surprised to see it was Woonsak who had grabbed him so roughly. Was Woonsak angry because George had overslept? "What's the matter?" George asked in the Indian language.

"You brave paleface papoose. You no go on this trip. Other paleface papoose, he go."

George's eyes widened as he stared at the tall Indian. He realized Woonsak was trying to tell him that Robert and he were to be separated. Robert would go with the braves on their trip, but George was to stay at camp. The thought that he and Robert might be separated had never come to him before. Who would look after poor, sick Robert?

"No, Woonsak. Robert is my friend. We go together."

Woonsak just shook his head and impatiently motioned for George to return to camp.

George slowly walked back to the wigwam and stood staring at Robert, who still lay where George had left him. George pulled him to his feet. "Come outside, Robert. You need the fresh air."

Robert stumbled out of the wigwam and then slumped to the ground.

"Robert, your pony is ready to go with the braves. But they won't let me get to my pony. They are going to separate us. Do you understand?"

Robert looked straight ahead, as though he had not heard.

"Robert, listen to me. I won't be with you anymore. But you'll be all right if you'll just act brave. You can if you try. You must eat the food they give you, and you must not cry."

Robert still looked away. "I might as well be talking Indian to him instead of English," George thought. "He just won't listen." The thought came to George that Robert would never live to escape with him. He would more likely die from not eating and from constantly crying.

Just then Woonsak appeared with two bowls of rabbit stew that had been boiling in big pots since dawn. He handed one bowl to George and the other to Robert. Then he stood watching the two pale-face boys. George immediately pulled a big chunk of rabbit from the bowl and bit into it. Robert laid the bowl on the ground.

"Eat," Woonsak said to Robert.

"That's plain enough," George thought. "He said it in English."

"I don't want it," Robert said.

"Eat!" Woonsak commanded, louder this time. Then, seeing that Robert wouldn't move, Woonsak picked up the bowl of stew, pulled Robert's head back by the hair, and forced the bowl to his lips. With a fierce grunt of anger, the Indian forced the stew into Robert's mouth, some of it going in but most of it spilling down the front of his already filthy shirt. Robert screamed and choked, but Woonsak forced him to drink more. Now other Indians gathered, and they cheered Woonsak on. He forced Robert to drink still more of the soup, until George thought his friend would choke to death. Finally, Woonsak jerked Robert to his feet, but Robert's legs crumpled under him. George covered his face with his hands and sobs shook his body.

Then he heard Robert call, "Go get your pony, George. Why don't you go get it? They are waiting for you, George!"

Lifting his head, George saw that the Indians were dragging Robert to his horse. Robert continued to call for George to get his horse, and George realized that Robert had not understood anything he had told him earlier about their being separated.

He ran wildly after Robert, and squaws turned to stare after this boy who usually seemed so calm. At the edge of the camp where the Indians were preparing to leave, George saw the Indians tying Robert to a pony. Then they mounted and started to ride, one brave leading Robert's pony.

"George! George!" Robert screamed.

The procession headed north, and George ran after them. "Don't scream, Robert," he beard himself say. "Don't cry, and remember to eat. Act brave, Robert. Please be brave!" But the galloping ponies soon outdistanced the running boy.

As the Indians turned a bend in the path, George saw one wave a tomahawk before Robert's face. Robert screamed the loudest scream George had ever heard. Then they were out of sight. George felt sure he would remember that terrified scream as long as he lived.

For the first time the Indians saw George cry out loud. When he returned to Woonsak's wigwam, he lay down on his blanket and cried himself to sleep. About noon he rose and went to the stream to wash his face. He spent the afternoon walking in the edge of the woods that skirted the camp, and most of the time he continued to cry. George decided that he could never, never like the Indians. They had made his life miserable, stealing him away from his family and then separating him from his best friend. "Maybe they've even killed Robert by now," he thought, and then began a fresh crying session.

42

George didn't eat any food that day, and he barely ate the next day. But on the third morning when he woke up, he began to realize how foolish he was acting.

"Why, I've done nothing but cry for two days," he thought. "And I used to tell Robert how useless it is to cry. I must be making these Indians as disgusted as Robert made them."

He rolled up his blanket and ran to the stream to wash. When he returned, he took the bowl of hominy that Woonsak's squaw offered him and quickly finished it. Then he ate a second bowl. George had not realized how hungry he was. Now he looked around the camp for Woonsak and realized he had not seen the big warrior since Robert left. What if Woonsak had gone too? Then he really would be alone.

"Where is Woonsak?" George asked Woonsak's squaw. He could put together simple sentences now in the Indian language and at least make himself understood.

"Woonsak, go on hunt for deer and birds. He be back in few days."

"Whew! At least Woonsak hasn't deserted me," George thought.

Then because he had nothing else to do he began to help the squaw with her work. First he helped her hang venison on poles to dry over a smoking fire. Then he helped her scrape the last of the meat from the deer hides. The squaw smiled at him happily and patted his head a few times.

George felt sorry that he had let the Indians see him cry. They would probably call him a papoose and a squaw. He decided that they would never see him cry again. From now on he would be strong no matter what happened. Wasn't that how Pa had always taught him to be?

Thinking of Pa brought his comfortable home and hardworking parents to mind with a sickening rush. What were they doing now? Did they think he was dead? What would Mrs. Stewart think of him if she knew he had let the Indians carry off Robert? Would she under-stand that he could do nothing about it?

More than anything, he wanted to escape from this dreary Indian camp. With his new feeling of strength and braveness came a kind of hardening to his heart. Everything he did from now on would be toward the purpose of escaping. First, he realized, he would have to find out for sure from the Indians if they killed his parents during the raid. Then he would have to find out in which direction his settlement lay. Finally, he would somehow have to find an opportunity to escape.

When Woonsak returned from the hunt, he was pleased to see George helping the squaw. "Woonsak will make little paleface brave a bow and arrows soon. Then paleface can go with Woonsak on hunt."

"Woonsak show me how to make bow and arrows and I will help him," George replied. George thought it might be a good thing to know for when he found his chance to escape.

"We passed through good hunting grounds on the way to this camp," George said. "Which way did we come?"

"We come from the south."

Then George knew that in order to return home he would have to travel south.

Weeks passed quickly now because Woonsak kept George busy. George helped the squaw tan the hide from the deer Woonsak caught on his last hunt. He helped her tend to the corn in the field, dug roots from the forest for her to mix in the venison stew, and sometimes even watched after her little papoose when she had to be away from the wigwam. George guessed that this papoose was only about two years old. Yet he already stood tall and was strong and plump, with shiny black eyes. The baby looked very much like his father, Woonsak, and George thought he would probably grow to be a great warrior too.

George often grew tired of doing squaw's work, and when Woon-

sak saw he looked bored, he would wave the boy away from the wigwam. "Go find other papooses," Woonsak would say, and George
would seek out the other boys his age and play.

As George ran about the camp, he learned to know most of the
Indian braves. Many of them acted kind toward him in a stern sort of
way. One day an old brave slipped up behind George and handed him
a beautiful whip made from plaited strands of buckskin of many bright
colors. Another day an Indian gave him a beaded belt. That same day
Woonsak took him to the field where the ponies grazed and told him
to catch the pony he had ridden on the way to camp. George spotted
the shiny brown and white pony on the other side of the field, caught
him, and rode him back to Woonsak. George had grown fond of this
sturdy animal that had carried him through the long journey. He knew
the pony was a favorite of the Indians, and they called him Neko.

"Neko, is yours," Woonsak said. "He is yours to keep."

"Mine? Whoopee!" George shouted and raced the pony around
the pasture, for a minute sounding like a wild Indian himself.

After that George spent many hours with Neko, feeding him,
grooming him, and riding him around and around the clearing. Sometimes he would trot the pony smartly through the camp. He sat as tall
and proud as the Indians and would loudly crack his new whip in the
air. He'd show these Indians that he was just as good a rider as the
Indian boys, maybe even better.

Soon after he had been given Neko, Woonsak had another gift for
George. He held out a new buckskin shirt and trousers and a pair of
delicately beaded moccasins.

"Woonsak's squaw make these for you because you help her do
work," Woonsak said.

This gift pleased George almost as much as the pony. He had worn
the same clothes since leaving his settlement, washing them occasion-

ally in the stream and enjoying a swim while they dried in the sun. But now they had big holes and were badly torn. George put on his new Indian clothes and paraded before Woonsak, who looked pleased. George knew that he looked like an Indian now, except for his light skin and hair.

"But," he told himself fiercely, "I am not an Indian. I am a white boy, the grandson of a colonist from Germany. My name is George Augustus Boylan, and I am not about to forget that."

Weeks turned into months, and as time passed George was given more freedom. One day he decided to explore a path that led toward the south, toward home. Every day he rode farther and farther along the path, and every day as he returned he saw an Indian scout watching him closely. "I will keep riding just a little farther every day," George decided. "Finally the scout will think I am just exercising Neko and he won't watch me so carefully. Then will be my chance."

But George realized that if he were to escape this year it would have to be very soon, for the weather would turn cold shortly. Woonsak's squaw had no calendar like Ma had, yet George could tell from the ripening wild fruit and the falling leaves from forest trees that it was nearly fall. They had even harvested the corn a few weeks ago.

He still didn't know if his parents lived, but even if they didn't he would still want to escape. He could always go back to Germantown and live with Grandpa and Grandma Boylan.

One day he rode Neko down the path that went south. He wore his warm Indian clothes, had an extra blanket packed on Neko, and carried the bow and arrows Woonsak had shown him how to make. When he came to the fork in the path where he had always turned back before, he stopped. Then he chose the path that led toward the southeast and rode on. He rode slowly, for if any Indians were watching, he would not want them to be suspicious. Yet he had not seen the usual scout today. He rode what he figured must be a mile from the camp, then another half mile. Now he was coming to a small hill. He kicked Neko, with both heels and rode hard up the hill.

Then on another higher hill to the right he saw the Indian scout. The Indian sat quietly on his pony, watching George with an expressionless face. George pretended not to see the scout and rode a little farther. Then as if he had grown tired of the ride, he pulled Neko to a halt, stretched his arms, and turned back toward the camp.

When he reached the wigwam, Woonsak's hard black eyes looked at him coldly. "The scout must have reached here before me," George thought. "Little paleface ride too far today," Woonsak said. "Little paleface might get lost. Paleface stay close to camp."

George nodded his head obediently and walked inside the wigwam. That night he heard another powwow being held in the clearing. But the Indians talked softly, and he could not make out what they said. The next morning squaws were taking down wigwams and braves packed deerskin bags onto their ponies. George knew that they were breaking camp. He wondered why they should break camp so close to winter.

"Well, it's too late now to worry about it," he thought. "As long as we're traveling, there will be no chance to escape. I won't be able to go home this year. But there are always other years. These Indians can't keep their eyes on me forever."

Chapter 7

War Paint and Feathers

Colored leaves, red, yellow, and brown, fluttered past George as he rode behind Woonsak in the long string of Indians and ponies. They were riding north and moving quickly. So many Indians moved along the path that George, who rode near the front of the line, could not see the end when he turned around to look. The farther they went, the more unhappy George became. For with every step, Neko took him farther and farther from his home and from Ma and Pa. Even the fluttering leaves seemed like little hands waving good-bye all the day long.

No hint of sun shone in the clouded sky, and George shivered from the cold. When Woonsak had given him the new buckskin pants and shirt, they had seemed so warm. But it had been summer then, and now a harsh, chill wind blew.

When the Indians stopped in a large clearing about noon for a brief rest, George felt glad to stretch his legs. He jumped off Neko, and ran around the pony in little circles, trying to get warm. Then Woonsak came to him and removed the extra blanket George had strapped to Neko's back.

"Here, little paleface brother," Woonsak said. "This is how wise Indians keep warm."

Then he showed George how to wrap the blanket around himself and tuck in the corners so it would not fall off.

"Woonsak must teach you to be Indian. Where you go soon you

will want to be good Indian," Woonsak said. Then he walked away, leaving George to wonder what he meant.

"Where could they be taking me that I would want to be a good Indian? I am the son of a German and proud of it. Why should I want to be a good Indian?"

Before he had time to do more wondering, the Indians mounted their ponies, and Woonsak motioned for George to get on Neko. They continued on the northward path for hours. George occasionally took a piece of dried venison from his pack and chewed on it. He remembered how strange it had tasted to him that first day with the Indians. Now it tasted as familiar to him as Ma's flapjacks used to taste.

When dark began to set in, Woonsak reined in his pony and waited for George. "Little brave warm now?" he asked, putting his hand on the blanket around George's shoulders.

"Yes, it is better," George said. George had to admit to himself that the blanket was a wonderful help. He liked the way it cuddled over his shoulders, shutting the cold air away from his body. But he would not admit this to Woonsak.

To the Indian he said, "Ma used to make me warm jackets from buckskin lined with the wool of sheep. A fellow never felt cold when he wore one of them."

Woonsak made no reply but moved ahead to his place in the long line of Indians.

After a ride of three days, they arrived late one evening at a large clearing that showed signs of previous encampments. Little piles of charcoal littered the ground and here and there lay parts of wigwams. Woonsak told George they would be camping there a few days. George wondered why, but did not ask. He helped Woonsak and his squaw set up a temporary shelter and then gratefully rolled into his blankets and immediately fell asleep.

49

The next morning George awoke at about dawn to hear the sound of many pounding hooves galloping away from camp. He looked out the flap of Woonsak's shelter. Only the squaws and a few wrinkled old men remained in the camp. The old men sat around campfires as silent and still as boulders. They smoked long pipes and paid no attention when George asked where the younger braves had gone.

Then George spotted Woonsak's squaw and asked her.

"Paleface boy help me make fire and not ask so many questions," she said sternly, and George meekly obeyed.

After George ate stew that the squaw boiled over the fire, he decided to take Neko for a brief ride around the camp. He walked to the area where the ponies had been left and called for Neko. But Neko did not appear. Then he whistled his usual whistle, but still no Neko.

Why, they must have taken Neko with them. Now George felt lonelier than ever. What had caused them to go and leave him with the squaws and silent old men? Then a few days later, as unexpectedly as they had gone, the braves returned. They rode into camp, laughing and talking loudly. The ponies carried huge bundles that reminded George of the ones that had carried the goods stolen from his mother. As the Indians unloaded them he discovered they contained many things that only settlers could have made. Copper pots, pretty china, some of it broken now, men's and women's clothing, and the usual assortment of stolen silverware, clocks, vases, and candlesticks.

"Why, they've been on a raid and have stolen this stuff from some poor settlers," George thought. "That's why the squaws wouldn't tell me where they had gone and the old men wouldn't even listen to me!"

But just as the anger began to rise up inside him, George spotted his pony, Neko.

"Neko!" he shouted, and ran to the little spotted pony. George threw his arms around Neko's neck and pressed the smooth head against his own. "So they took you with them. Well, I won't blame you for what they did, because you couldn't help it. But if only you could talk. Then you could tell me where the settlement is and we could run there together."

Then George began walking among the Indians again, watching as they inspected their bundles. He noticed that some of these braves were strangers. They looked wilder and wore more war paint than the Indians of his camp. He moved closer to these visitors to get a better look and then stopped horrified. Each of them had scalps hanging from his beaded leather belt. Some of the scalps had short hair attached to them, some had curly hair, others had long wavy hair flowing from them.

George felt sick. He had to stuff his fist in his mouth to hold back the scream of horror that wanted to escape. Then Woonsak stood beside him and led him away. Woonsak had a big bundle in his hand. He pushed it toward George and urged him to open it. But George felt too weak to hold the sack and it dropped to the ground, spilling out boys' clothes of all kinds that looked to be his size—shoes, stockings, trousers, shirts, even a sturdy buckskin jacket.

"These are for you," Woonsak said and smiled gently, nudging George.

"Those stockings," George thought. "Some poor mother worked hard to knit them for her boy. And she worked to make him warm pants and shirts and that jacket. She worked on them for many days, even weeks."

Woonsak picked up the jacket and put it around George's trembling shoulders. Suddenly George was filled with such anger as he had never felt before. He flung the jacket from his shoulders to the ground. He cried out in sorrow and kicked at the bundle of clothes with all his might. The Indians around him stopped their work to stare at him. Some looked surprised, and others looked plainly displeased, especially the visiting Indians.

George looked around him at the strange Indian faces and knew he had to escape. He began to run from them, heading for the woods, tears streaming down his face. He heard pounding footsteps coming quickly behind and tried to run faster. But instead he stumbled over the big roots of a tree and fell. Now strong arms grabbed him from behind and hit him several hard blows across the side of his head. George put his hands up to try to protect his head and kicked at his captor with both feet. Then the warm blanket was pulled from his shoulders.

With a mighty twist, George pulled free of the strong hands and turned to face the angry Indian, whom he recognized as one from Woonsak's tribe. "I don't care!" George screamed at the Indian. "I don't want your dirty old blanket anyway. I hate it!"

The Indian just threw the blanket over his own shoulder and dragged struggling George back to Woonsak's shelter. George immediately took off the beaded moccasins and threw them with his whip and belt at Woonsak's feet. His Indian friend looked at him sadly but did not say a word. Not knowing what else to do, George then stepped inside the shelter and lay down to sleep. But cold winds blew into the shelter, and George could not sleep for shivering. He had no blanket to wrap himself in, and his shirt and pants were not thick enough to keep out the cold. He tried to think over what had just happened, but sleepiness finally overtook him.

The next morning George woke up to find his blanket, moccasins, whip, and belt lying by his side. Woonsak must have brought them to him. Now he felt a little ashamed for the way he had acted. But as he continued to think about it, he decided he had done the right thing. At least these Indians would know that he hated killing and stealing. Ma and Pa would want him to show this by the way he lived. "Except," he thought, "I guess I could have found a more grown-up way to show it."

When he sat up, he saw Woonsak sitting on the ground nearby. The Indian did not smile, but he motioned for George to put the moccasins and blanket back on. George gladly obeyed, for he felt cold and stiff. His arms even looked blue. He ate a bowl of stew offered him by Woonsak's squaw and then picked up his belt and whip and headed for the pony corral. Once on Neko's sturdy back, George felt better. He knew the Indians would be watching him, so he was careful to keep in sight of camp.

"I wish you could tell me where you have been, Neko," George whispered to his pony as he had done the day before. "I know it wasn't your fault. You're a prisoner just like I am. You didn't want to go on the raid, did you, Neko? Oh, I hope we can run away together someday. But we'll have to wait for the warm weather now. Snow will soon cover the ground, and we couldn't possibly make it then."

George was glad to see, when he returned to camp, that the visiting Indians had left. They made him feel like Shep, his dog at home. Every time he saw war paint and feathers, George wanted to snarl and growl.

The Indians broke camp again the next morning, and once more George found himself riding miles each day, from sunup until long after sundown. Now Woonsak used the time they traveled to teach George more of the Indian language. They spent long hours together each day going over and over the Indian words. George learned fast, and soon he could understand almost anything the Indians said to him, and to their surprise they could understand most of the Indian words he spoke.

Sometimes when he saw that George had grown tired of riding, Woonsak would take him aside and point out something interesting in the woods. He showed George how the squirrels stored food in holes of big trees for the winter. He pointed out caves where bears slept for their long winter hibernation. One time he led George to a little lake. Trees had been felled across the water. George looked at the stumps and asked if someone had been there and cut down the trees. "Perhaps a white settler has been here," George thought. "Maybe Woonsak will trade me for some warm blankets or a few animals."

"No, little brave," Woonsak said. "No man did this. Look at the right bank of the lake."

What George saw was a big mound of branches and dirt with a little animal moving about on it. George had never come across such an animal before. It had a tail shaped like a flat shovel, and it was busily working mud into the walls of its lodge.

As quietly as a leaf falls, Woonsak crept forward, close to the animal. George followed. "This must be a beaver," George decided. Pa had told him about beavers and how they build homes, and dams across water, of mud and tree branches.

"Little animal is building his own wigwam," Woonsak whispered. "He will live there with his family."

Once more Woonsak turned and quietly walked back through the trees. George turned to go too, but this time he stepped on a fallen branch and it crackled. George looked quickly at the beaver to see if he had scared it. At once the animal looked up, poised and alert. It eyed George for a second, then dived gracefully into the water.

Day after day the Indian party continued to travel. George grew sore from riding long hours, and when they did stop to rest once or twice a day, he could hardly walk. At night, after it had grown dark, they hastily made camp, building fires around which they all crowded trying to get warm. If a hunter had been lucky that day, they ate boiled squirrel or rabbit, or turkey roasted over the fire. Sometimes they even had fresh roasted venison. But other days, when luck had been poor, they had to satisfy their hungry stomachs with the black dried venison and roots pulled from the forest.

George usually felt so tired he would collapse into his blanket as soon as he had eaten, and fall asleep. And often he had the same dream. He would see himself running as hard as he could along paths through the woods. After a while he would come to paths that looked familiar and realize they led to his home settlement. Then through the trees he would spy the smooth peeled logs of Pa's cabin. He'd run toward it and with trembling hands unlatch the wooden yard gate. As he ran for the cabin door, it would start to open. But at this point, George always woke up. Realizing that it had all been a dream and he still lay in the open air, shivering from the cold, he would quietly cry himself back to sleep.

Riding on farther into the clearing with the Indians,
George saw a huge village of wigwams on the shore of the big lake.
Was this to be the end of his journey?

Chapter 8

Son of Chief Big Wolf

As the Indians continued to travel hard without letup, George wondered if they would ever reach wherever they had set out for. He imagined that they would ride on and on until he finally dropped from Neko's back to the hard ground.

"How much farther must we go?" George would call ahead to Woonsak. But the Indian always continued to look straight ahead as though he had not heard.

But one day as they rode through an area particularly thick with trees and bushes, George's sharp eyes caught the light of a clearing up ahead. Clearings had been few in this section of the woods, so he felt anxious to see what it would be. Then he rode onto a low hill that lay directly before the clearing and the sight that met him took George totally by surprise.

A vast body of deep blue water, stretching as far as he could see, lay before him. At first George thought it must be the ocean. But then he remembered that Pa always said the ocean roared louder than a bear and had mighty waves that foamed white with salt. This water lay still, quietly shimmering in the glow of late afternoon sun. No, this must be one of the big northern lakes his schoolmaster back in Germantown had talked about. The teacher had said that five of them lay in the area near Canada and had pointed on the map to show how big they were.

"Anyway," George thought, "I know we've been riding north, and this certainly is the biggest lake I've ever seen."

Then, far down the shore of the lake, George saw something he had not noticed before—a huge Indian village. Indians swarmed among long lodges and smaller wigwams. Squaws bent over fires tending to their cooking, and children seemed to be running everywhere. George noticed something particularly strange near the center of the village. Dozens and dozens of Indian boys about George's age seemed to be playing in a huge oval almost as large as the rest of the village and surrounded by a low dirt wall. The boys ran, jumped, wrestled, and performed stunts of all kinds on the oval's smooth dirt floor. George couldn't imagine why the boys ran around as they did, yet he wished he could be in the oval playing with them. Now George looked up to discover that the rest of his group had ridden ahead, so he dug his heels into Neko's flanks and rode hard to catch up. Shouts of welcome came from the village when the people caught sight of the returning party. And the braves returned the shouts with whoops and hollers. George thought he had never heard such noise in all his life. After the shouting had died down, the village people began looking around to see what the braves had brought home with them. That's when they discovered George.

George had ridden a little to one side, watching the excitement. Then an old squaw gave a weird cry and pointed her bony finger toward the paleface boy on his pony. The people began moving toward him, and he soon found himself surrounded by noisy squaws and children. George guessed he must be an odd sight to them. Though he had become tan from the sun and wind, his skin still looked paler than theirs. And, much to his disgust, his light hair had grown and now lay in curly ringlets on his shoulders. He supposed that many of the Indians had never seen any kind of hair except their own straight black hair.

At first the squaws just looked and pointed at him. Then a few reached up dirty hands to touch his light face and run their fingers through his curly hair. George sat still, thinking he would let them look until they grew tired and went away. But all at once he felt four strong hands lift him bodily from Neko's back. The next thing be knew he was being passed bodily from squaw to squaw as though he were a weak papoose. One would pull his arm in one direction and another his leg in the opposite direction, all trying to look at him at once. They laughed and chattered, but George had become so upset he couldn't understand a word they said.

Now George was scared. What did they want to do with him? Did they feel his arms and legs to see if he felt fat enough to eat? Did they run their fingers through his hair because they wanted it for a scalp?

Then a tall, handsome Indian man, dressed in beautifully beaded buckskin pants and shirt, stepped before the circle of women. They instantly became quiet and dropped George to the ground. The man took George by the shoulder and led him toward the village, past the oval where the boys stopped playing to stare at George, and on to a huge wigwam. George saw that this wigwam stood taller than any others in the village. Bright designs of beads and trinkets decorated the sides.

The Indian lifted a soft black bearskin which served as the wigwam door and gently pushed George inside. As his eyes became used to the dimness of the wigwam, George noticed piles of heavy blankets heaped to one side. Soft skins covered the floor and felt warm under his feet. Now he looked into the face of the Indian who had brought him here. The Indian stood tall and straight with great muscles bulging beneath the rough sleeves of his shirt. George had never seen broader shoulders. Not a muscle moved in the Indian's strong bronze face, but when George met his eyes they glowed like live coals. Yet the deeply lined face did not look evil or unkind. After a few more seconds, the Indian turned and walked out of the wigwam, leaving George alone.

59

George ran his fingers over the walls, and they felt soft and smooth. Looking closely, he saw they were made from many animal skins sewed together so skillfully that they seemed to be one piece. George noticed, too, that this wigwam was kept neat and clean.

A huge bearskin hung from the side of the wigwam, and as George gazed at it he noticed it seemed to move as though it were alive. A little chill of fear ran through George. Someone was hidden behind that skin watching him! Then a corner of the skin was pushed aside and there stood a little Indian maiden.

The girl stood so still that she resembled a wooden statue more than a human being, and George was amazed at how pretty she looked. Her big black eyes stared steadily at him without blinking. Her face was small-featured with high cheekbones and red lips. She had strands of colored beads braided into her long black hair, and she wore a beaded deerskin dress. Tiny moccasins covered her feet.

But George did not have long to gaze at this unexpected vision, for an old wrinkled hand poked out from behind the rug and snatched the little girl out of sight.

"Who is that pretty little girl?" he wondered. "What is she doing here? And what am I doing here?"

He suddenly felt too tired to care. Nobody had been unkind to him, and this place felt warm and comfortable. Why should he worry? The heap of blankets looked inviting after the many days of hard riding. Abruptly, he lay down on them and soon fell fast asleep.

A few hours later George was awakened by hands tugging at his shirt. He woke to stare into the faces of two Indian squaws. He saw that one held a round pot and something moved in it like liquid.

"Maybe they have brought me some food," George thought. And he realized that he did indeed feel very hungry.

But the squaw set the pot on the floor and joined the other one who still tugged at his shirt.

"What are you doing?" George yelled in English. Then realizing they could not understand, he repeated it in Indian: "What are you doing?"

The squaws looked at one another and giggled. "We make you look like fine Indian," one of them said.

Then they began in earnest to remove his clothes. George kicked and twisted, but the squaws were stronger than he, and they soon had him undressed. Then the one picked up her pot while the other held him down. She dipped a white cloth into the pot and the cloth came out brown. Then she quickly smoothed the cloth over his body and George felt shocked to see his own skin turn brown.

"Hey! Stop that. What do you think you're doing? You're ruining my skin!" George protested in vain, for the squaws just worked all the harder. When they had finished staining him brown, they cut off his long hair. Reaching his hand to his head, George could feel only a narrow strip of short, stubby hair going from his forehead to the nape of his neck. Then they swabbed this with their stain and turned it as black as they could make it.

"You've turned me into an Indian!" George said sadly, poking a brown arm toward one of them.

But the squaws paid no attention and soon had him dressed in a new pair of buckskin pants and a beaded buckskin shirt. Then with a satisfied smile they led him outside to the Indian who had brought him to this wigwam. The Indian sat cross-legged on the ground, smoking a pipe that had a long, feathered handle. He slowly pulled the pipe from his mouth and looked George over carefully from head to foot. Then he gave a grunt of approval. "I am Big Wolf, chief of this tribe," the Indian said. "Many moons ago my squaw died and left me with Ewanah, my girl papoose and the light of my heart. But she left me no boy papoose. Big Wolf has need of a son. From now on, you are my son! You must always be strong and brave. You must be a good Indian, learning to do things better than all other Indian boys. And you must become a mighty warrior and leader of people."

Then Big Wolf fell silent and with a wave of his hand, dismissed George. George was amazed to learn that he had become son of an Indian chief. Was this why he had been stolen from Ma and Pa in the first place? So the chief could have a son? And had the Indians forced the long ride to this village in cold weather because the chief was anxious to see his new son? George wondered if the chief felt pleased with him. But he figured he would probably never know for certain the answers to these questions. He walked into the village and tried to decide what to do. He had never felt more out of place. He knew that his skin and hair and even his clothes now made him look Indian, but in his heart he felt he could never really be an Indian. He looked at one bronzed arm and then the other and felt sad. Ma and Pa wouldn't even recognize him!

"Do not look so fearful, little brave." A familiar voice spoke behind him, and George turned to face Woonsak.

"Oh, Woonsak, where have you been? Look what they have done to me!" George stuck out an arm for Woonsak to see.

Woonsak smiled. "That is only dye from some roots of the forest. It will come off soon and have to be done again. It will have to be done many, many times so long as you live."

This made George feel better. At least underneath the paint, he was still a German boy.

"Since you are son of Big Wolf, you must look like an Indian."

"But I don't want to be son of Big Wolf. I want to stay with you."

"You will like being son of Big Wolf. He is a mighty chief and a brave warrior. He is good, and his people love him. You, too, will love

Big Wolf."

George wanted to shout that he could never love being the son of these Indians who lived so differently from what he was used to and who had stolen him away from Ma and Pa. But he knew that he must not dare say such a thing, so he said nothing.

"Woonsak will be near. My wigwam is on the other side of the village. Sometimes Woonsak will come to see you."

Just then a wrinkled old squaw came up to George and led him away. On the other side of the squaw walked the little Indian maiden George had seen in the wigwam. George guessed by now that she was Ewanah, the daughter Big Wolf had mentioned. Ewanah held tightly to the squaw's hand and peeked around her skirts at George.

They stopped by the wigwam of Big Wolf and sat down by the outdoor cook fire. The chief soon joined them, and the squaw dished up a big pot of venison stew. While Big Wolf ate he lifted chunks of lean meat from the pot, pulled off the choicest bits, and popped them into the mouths of George and Ewanah. The little girl was obviously used to this attention from her father, but George hardly knew what to do.

As they ate, the old squaw watched them closely, dishing up more meat and corn or handing them a bit of cloth to wipe their greasy fingers on. But she did not eat. Like all good Indian squaws, she waited until the others had eaten. Then she would feed herself from what was left.

When they had finished the stew, the squaw handed each one a flat cake baked to a tasty brown. George bit into it, and it tasted like the corn cakes his mother sometimes made by mixing pounded corn with milk, fat, and leavening.

"Is this not the best food young brave has eaten?" the chief asked proudly.

"It is very good."

"Young brave will have many good things to eat, and he will always have warm clothes, many bows and arrows, and swift ponies."

"Oh, but I have a pony. A brown-and-white one named Neko."

"Big Wolf's son will have many ponies!"

After the chief took his last bite of cake, he rose and walked into the village. The squaw led George inside the wigwam and pointing to the blankets said, "Sleep!" Then she left him alone.

George did not feel like sleeping. He gazed around at his new home and was again surprised to see how clean it looked. Ma would feel better if she could know he lived in such a nice clean place. Maybe this business of being a chief's son wouldn't be so bad after all!

George leaned back on the blankets and without realizing it fell asleep. He awoke later and found little Ewanah staring down at him.

"Hello," George said in the Indian language he had learned.

"Hello," she said shyly.

"Do you live in this wigwam, too?"

"No. You live here with Big Wolf. You are my brother. I love you."

This statement surprised George, and he jumped when he heard another voice behind him.

"Ewanah lives with me in wigwam across from this wigwam." George did not even have to turn around to recognize the crackly voice of the old squaw. "This wigwam is the home of Big Wolf. Now it is your home too." The squaw stood up and laid some blankets on top of a pile of skins by one wall. "The night is dark now. You will sleep here," she said to George, pointing to the skins. Then she led Ewanah outside.

When George lay down on the skins, he found they made a bed as soft as the feather mattress on Ma and Pa's bed. He remembered how good that mattress had felt to him when the hatchet had flown off its handle and struck his head. He reached up a hand and ran his fingers across the ridgy scar, barely hidden by his close-cropped hair.

Thinking of that featherbed made him feel a little homesick, and once again he told himself that he would someday escape.

"But I must not let being a chief's son make me forget who I am," he reminded himself. "I am George Augustus Boylan, and whatever Indian name they give me I will still know who I really am!"

Chapter 9

Fight in the Oval Arena

George woke up with a comfortable feeling. Several days had passed since he first arrived in the Indian village, and they had been days of fun and new experiences. Every day he went fishing in the big lake with some Indian boys about his age. Sometimes he galloped Neko along the lake shore. He spent long hours watching the squaws tan deer and coon hides and sew them together. And when he grew tired of that, he would explore the huge village, getting acquainted with its many paths and the layout of the wigwams. But best of all, for the first time in weeks he went to bed with a full stomach, slept soundly at night, and woke up mornings feeling warm and snug on a pile of soft skins and covered with thick Indian blankets.

Now he jumped up, gathered his new buckskin clothes, and hurried to a stream that ran near the rear of the wigwam he shared with Big Wolf. He washed quickly, for the early morning air chilled him and the water felt colder yet. Returning from the stream and feeling fresh and clean, he spotted Ewanah tussling happily with a large brown-and-white spotted dog. The dog towered above the little girl, but he seemed friendly and obviously didn't mind when she hugged him, pulled at his tail, or rolled with him on the ground.

"It is the little girl," George whispered. "Ewanah." He had grown fond of this child in the few days he had known her. At first Ewanah had been shy, but she was not anymore. Just the day before, when he had stooped down to take a stone from his moccasin, she had jumped onto his back quick as a flash. She threw her arms tightly around his neck and he had run with her around the village, the two of them laughing, and the squaws they passed nodding their heads in approval.

"I'll see if she wants another ride," George thought; but as he drew near the little girl, something unexpected happened. The dog stopped playing with Ewanah and turned to face George. The hair on the back of his neck stood up, and he growled threateningly, showing big teeth. Now the dog crouched between Ewanah and George, a low snarling growl rumbling in his throat.

"Do not move closer if you want to stay alive," a voice said from behind George. It was an Indian brave who lived in a nearby wigwam, but the brave did not seem to know what to do about the angry dog. Ewanah and her old squaw ran to the dog, both of them scolding him at once. The dog stopped growling, and George moved closer. Now the dog knew George was a friend, and George joined Ewanah in playing with the big animal. After that George had a new friend. The dog often followed him around the village and seemed to feel that he must take care of George just as he guarded Ewanah.

Later that morning as George watched some squaws work with deer hides, Big Wolf appeared beside him. Since George seldom saw the chief except during meals and sometimes in the early morning, he felt surprised at this appearance.

"Come with me," Big Wolf commanded, and George followed. They walked along winding village paths until they came to the big oval area where George had seen young Indians playing that first day in the village. Boys of all ages ran, jumped, wrestled, and played in the oval today as they had then. Big Wolf sat down on a log and watched and George did the same. He watched as the boys raced, jumped, wrestled, and boxed. Sometimes he burst out laughing at the clever tactics the boys used in getting the best of their opponents, and the chief seemed pleased with George. Then George forgot himself completely while watching two nearby wrestlers. He judged them to be about his age.

"Why, that doesn't look hard," he thought. "It kind of looks like fun. I bet I could even teach them a thing or two."

The next thing George knew two hands pushed him roughly from behind, and he was sent sprawling, face down in the dusty oval. As he turned over and struggled to stand up, a moccasined foot struck against his chest, and he again fell to the ground, so hard this time that bits of sand ground into the palm of his hand. Surprised and angered, George sprang up and found himself facing one of the boys he had been fishing with earlier in the morning. The boy squatted down, ready to lunge at George again, his bold bronze arms seesawing from tough, sturdy shoulders.

"Boy! Of all the nerve," George thought. "To attack me from behind! Well, I guess I'll teach him a good lesson he'll never forget!"

George sprang at the young Indian's face, but the Indian stepped lightly aside, and for the third time George found himself flat on the ground. When he turned around, the Indian boy watched him closely, making no moves until George moved. George leaped toward the Indian again, and in the next few minutes learned that he was no match for this fighter. The Indian twisted and turned, avoiding most of George's thrusts, but managing to make all of his own find George. George began to feel sure that the Indian had as many legs as a spider. The air seemed full of them and of slashing arms and pounding fists. Now George felt wet blood trickling from a cut on his face, and his lip felt as big as one of his ears. He felt like crying and running from this tough Indian, but then he remembered his father's warnings:

"If you should ever run afoul of the Indians, don't act scared. Do you hear me? Never, never show fear."

So George continued to fight the Indian until he felt he could take no more. Then he just stepped back and folded his hands on his chest. The other boy stepped back too. The Indian smiled at him, and George returned the smile, though it was a crooked smile and hurt a little.

Now George remembered Big Wolf, and turning around, found the chief watching him. He also had a grim smile on his face. Big Wolf said a few low words, and the boys who had gathered to watch scattered immediately. George stood still a few minutes, ashamed that Big Wolf had seen him beaten. Then he began to feel angry with himself. He quickly turned and walked away. He strode to the lake and washed his face and hands, holding the cold water to his eyes, nose, and mouth. Then he sat down on a log to think things over.

George tried to excuse himself. "He caught me when I wasn't looking!" But he knew that was not all. The boy's fists had been like steel, and he had danced and swerved to dodge every returned blow. The Indian knew how to fight.

"The thing for me to do is to practice jumping and running and wrestling like the other boys do," he thought. "Then I'll show them I'm as tough as they are. And I'll start learning right away."

Now the thought came to George that Big Wolf must have planned this match just to show George how much training he needed. He determined to practice and exercise so that Big Wolf could feel proud of his adopted boy. The afternoon sun shone high in the sky though a cold wind whipped the air. But still George continued to sit on the log and think.

First he thought about his friend Robert, and George understood more than ever why Pa had reared him to be a man and not give in to pain and discomfort.

"I guess Robert's mother didn't know that by pampering and babying him she was really doing him harm," George thought. "If she

69

had known, she would have almost died herself."

Then George began to think of his own ma and pa, and he wished with all his heart to be home again in his nice comfortable settlement where a boy didn't have to worry about being a great wrestler or jumper. He wondered why he had to be separated from Ma and Pa, and why people had to suffer and even die though they were good people. All at once George wondered why God had let this unhappiness come to him. He had been good; he had prayed, read sometimes from the big family Bible, and even gone every week to the church when he lived in Germantown.

What was it Pa had always said about suffering? He said never to question God when things go wrong.

"God doesn't cause the suffering," Pa had said. "But when things do go wrong, He does help us endure. And He has promised a great reward if we live right and keep our faith."

"I will!" George said loudly into the forest, and a little gray squirrel sitting nearby cocked his head to listen. "I will keep my faith in God. I won't forget that He loves me, no matter what happens. After all, there are a lot of children who have faced worse problems than I have."

Now George was speaking so loudly that the squirrel grew frightened and ran away. When George realized he had been talking out loud, he sat back down on the log, feeling rather foolish, and continued thinking quietly. "But I haven't talked very much to God lately," he admitted. "I guess I've done too much worrying and not enough praying.

George resolved then and there that he would pray often for God's help, and he felt sure that God would find some way to help him.

"Even though it seems impossible now that I could ever escape from here, I know God will somehow help me find a way to get back home to my settlement."

Then George spotted Big Wolf coming toward him through the forest. The big Indian looked tall and strong and kind. He walked proudly and held his mouth in a firm, straight line, but his black eyes showed concern for the boy sitting on the log.

"Big Wolf has been good to me," George thought. "I must be good and obedient to him as long as I remain in this village. I must make him proud of me. I will obey him just so he never asks me to do something mean or wicked."

Big Wolf sat down on the log beside George. "The forest looks pretty now with the colored leaves. Soon it will be filled with snow, and ice will cover the tree branches like the clear glass I have seen used for windows."

George did not know what to say, so he said nothing. Big Wolf turned to face George and passed his rough hand gently over George's battered face. "The eyes are turning black," Big Wolf said. "Come. Follow me."

George followed Big Wolf to their wigwam, and the chief tied a piece of fresh venison to George's swollen eyes. The meat felt cool, and George lay back to rest.

A short time later the old squaw called George to the campfire outside. Rich, savory smells came from the pots she was stirring, and George suddenly felt very hungry. But when the squaw handed him a bowl of meat and vegetables, George found that he could not open his mouth wide enough to get the food inside. The squaw reached to take the bowl from him. "But I am hungry!" George protested.

Big Wolf looked amused. "Give her the bowl," he said, "and she will get you something that is easier to eat. The trouble is that the stomach does not know when the mouth is sore."

Even George had to laugh at that. Little Ewanah came and cud-

71

dled next to him, reaching her hand lightly to his bruised lip. Tears stood in her pretty eyes. George gratefully drank a bowl of broth, and he was surprised at how much better the warm liquid made him feel.

After supper George limped to his wigwam and tried to sleep. The squaw came with a poultice of pounded leaves for his lip. At first George yelled from the sting, but the squaw stubbornly continued to apply it. He found that the poultice soon soothed the pain, and within a few minutes he was fast asleep.

George started from the line as quickly as an arrow leaves its bow. The Indian remained behind. "Swift Arrow!" someone called.

Chapter 10

Swift Arrow

George awoke next morning feeling eager to get to the big oval arena for a real workout. The old squaw's poultice had done such a good job that he scarcely felt the cuts and bruises that resulted from yesterday's wrestling match. But when he told his plan to Big Wolf, the chief refused to let him go to the arena.

"Your eye is still swollen and black. Your lip is still cut and bruised. The gash on your cheek has not yet healed. You will wait until your face is better." And without waiting to hear George's protests, the chief walked into the village. What could George do but obey? The chief did not mention the arena again for a whole week, and George felt afraid to bring up the subject for fear of making him angry.

Then one evening as George sat brooding in the wigwam, Big Wolf again came to him. "Does young brave wish to try the arena again?"

"With Big Wolf's permission I will go back to the arena and learn to race and jump and wrestle as the other boys do. Then I will make Big Wolf proud."

The chief looked steadily at him, and once more George noticed how the man's eyes could glow like live coals. "When young son returns to the arena, he must be watchful and brave. He must know everything that is happening around him. When young brave has learned this lesson, then special teachers will train him to wrestle, run, jump, and hunt."

75

"Special teachers?" George repeated. Why should he need special teachers?

"Yes. As the chief's son, you must have special teachers. All chiefs' sons have special teachers. You must become the bravest, strongest, and toughest of all warriors." Again without waiting for anything more that George might want to say, Big Wolf turned and walked from the wigwam.

A messenger from the chief came to George the next day, and George followed him to the oval arena, where the chief waited. As soon as George came into view, the boys in the arena set up a loud, continuing war whoop. The sound of it brought back the memory of his last painful experience here and the thought filled him with dread and fear. But then he again remembered the many warnings from his father not to show fear in front of the Indians. So George walked bravely, with his head high and careful to hide the fluttering of his heart. Big Wolf nodded his head with a grim look of approval.

The closer George came to the arena, the more uproarious grew the shouts from the boys. But George continued to walk firmly and quietly, carefully surveying the scene with a calm face. He saw that the shouts came from about a hundred boys who had gathered to watch him. Then the chief turned his back to George and sat down upon a little hill. The other boys immediately resumed their activities in the arena.

"What am I supposed to do now?" George wondered. "The least Big Wolf could do is tell me what he expects."

Then George remembered Pa once saying, "Learn to think things through before you get into difficulties. I won't always be around to help you." "That certainly came true quicker than either of us ever expected," George thought sadly. "Pa is nowhere around here, and Big Wolf sure doesn't intend to give me any help now. He's just waiting to see what I'll do myself."

George moved a few steps ahead of the chief, and sat down on the ground by the arena. Two boys were wrestling furiously just a few yards away from him, and George decided that by watching them he could learn to wrestle without the help of those teachers Big Wolf insisted on.

"This is a pretty good place to sit," George assured himself. "No-body can get me here. Big Wolf's behind me, and he won't let any-body grab me from the rear."

Then George gave his whole attention to the wrestlers, thinking he'd learn some pointers in a hurry. He noted how they dodged and turned to avoid one another's kicks and thrusts. And he was amazed at how strong they were and the amount of pounding they could take. Within a few minutes George was totally engrossed, forgetting every-thing else around him.

Suddenly the light was blotted out as a rough hand clamped hard over George's eyes. Other hands were grabbing his feet, and the next thing he knew he was dropped headfirst into a vile smelling leather bag. It happened just as neatly as Ma used to plop a pillow into one of her clean, hand-woven pillow slips. George cried out angrily and struggled to turn himself upright. He thrashed out with his arms and legs. He even tried to bite his way through the bag but only ended up with a tongue full of dirty hairs. Despite all his thrashing, he was still upside down in the bag and his neck felt as though it would break in two. He finally wore himself out and lay quiet, but uncomfortable, in the bag. He could tell that he was being carried around and around, and he heard rude shouts of laughter coming from the young braves who he imagined had once more stopped their games to watch him be made a fool.

"Oh, why didn't I keep a more careful watch?" George asked himself. "Whatever made me think that Big Wolf would do my watching for me from the rear? Didn't he tell me yesterday that I must be alert to all things?"

Now George noticed that the cries from the arena were growing faint, and whoever carried him no longer tossed him about so roughly. They must be taking him someplace else, but where? Finally the sack was set down on the ground, and George crawled backward to get out. At first he could not see in the dimness. Then he gradually realized that he was back in his own wigwam. He rubbed his eyes. Whoever had carried him there had already disappeared, and so had the sack.

He looked to the doorway and found Big Wolf standing there, his arms folded across his heaving chest, and his eyes glaring at George with a scornful look. Big Wolf continued to stare at him for a long time, and George wished he could get back into that hateful sack to hide himself and his shame.

Finally the chief spoke. "Chief's son is like a weak rabbit. He thinks he is brave, but he will not be watchful. Chief's son is a papoose!" Then he disappeared through the doorway of the wigwam, leaving George alone.

For several days George felt too ashamed to venture outside. He often heard Ewanah playing nearby, but he did not join her. Once each day the old squaw brought him some food and water, but she said not a word to him. When Big Wolf came in at night to sleep, George would pretend that he was already asleep to avoid facing the disappointed chief.

One day the chief again sent for George, and he followed the messenger back to the arena. Another man stood beside the chief, a man who looked almost as sturdy and strong as the chief. George soon learned that this man was to be his special teacher, and George felt grateful that he would at least have someone to tell him what he was expected to do.

Big Wolf shouted a short command toward the arena, and a boy emerged from the group of playing braves. George recognized him as the same boy he had wrestled with the first time. The boy gave George a quick smile, but George thought it looked more like a sneer.

"It is as though he were saying, 'Here is one I can step on as easily as a baby owl,'" George told himself. "Well, I must do better today."

The teacher looked down at George and quickly rattled off a sharp command. But he spoke so rapidly that George could not understand. Seeing George's blank look, the teacher then repeated the same words to the other boy. The boy immediately seized George's arm and twisted it behind his back. He let go, and the teacher again gave the command to George. Now George understood what to do. He seized the other boy's arm and twisted it just as his own had been twisted behind his back.

Now the teacher gave another command, and the boy stepped forward and threw George lightly to the ground. He did it two more times, and then the teacher gave the command to George. George leaped toward the other boy and threw him to the ground using the same hold that the boy had used to throw him. And so the lesson continued. First the teacher would command the Indian boy to throw George with a particular hold. Then George would throw the boy with the same hold. George learned quickly, and he could tell from their expressions that both the teacher and the chief were pleased with him. Using the other boy as a model, the teacher showed George how to take hold of an opponent, what moves to make, how to dodge thrusts and blows, and how to gain the advantage. He directed the other boy to put holds on George and then showed George how to break them. After about two hours of this grueling lesson, George felt so tired he thought he would drop. But the other boy, being used to rough and tumble games, showed no signs of tiredness.

"I won't let them know how tired I am if it kills me," George thought. But just when he decided he could not take it a minute longer, the chief directed the teacher to stop the lesson. George sank gratefully to the ground and began to watch the others play. This time, however, he kept a careful watch on all sides. And when his wrestling opponent rushed quietly at him from behind, George was ready. At first he pretended he did not see, then at the last moment George leaped aside and the Indian sprawled in the dirt. The boy looked surprised when he stood up, then he grinned and slapped George heartily across the shoulder.

"Come, friend, I think we should run a race together," the boy said. George groaned inwardly, for he felt very tired; but he knew he must not show his weariness. He rose to his feet, and the teacher suggested that they race clear around the arena. At least running was a sport that George knew something about. Hadn't he been the fastest runner for his age in their settlement at home? And even in Germantown he had often beaten the older boys in races. For once George felt confident.

"I will show the chief that I am good for something," George muttered as the two boys stood at the starting line. Another boy shouted the signal for them to begin, and George started out with a mighty burst of speed. Already he had left his companion far behind.

"Swift Arrow!" he heard someone shout, and he felt pleased with himself. But then he heard the others laughing loudly, and he wondered what could be so funny. Should he not feel proud that he could start a race as swiftly as an arrow leaves the bow?

George felt that his feet were fairly flying around the arena. He continued going full speed; but about halfway around he had to slow up a bit, for his heart thumped loudly and his breath was beginning to come in short gasps. This was certainly the longest track he had ever run. Now George's feet moved slower and slower, and he wondered if he would ever make it to the finish line. Then he noticed that his opponent had gained on him. He came steadily on with long, loping steps that seemed not to wear him out. The boy passed George about three quarters of the way around the track and then sped up to an easy finish. George stumbled over the goal line, winded and exhausted, several seconds later.

Once more George felt ashamed because of a foolish performance. But he held his head high and smiled weakly at the victor. Then he turned and strode quickly toward his wigwam. Halfway home, Big Wolf overtook him, and George expected the chief to be angry again. But this time Big Wolf looked at him kindly.

"Swift Arrow can run fast," Big Wolf said. "Now he will learn to control his pace, and he will soon be a mighty runner."

"Swift Arrow?" George asked.

"Yes, Swift Arrow. Is that not a good name for one who starts a race so quickly? From now on you will be known as Swift Arrow!"

Chapter 11

Ewanah's Log Cabin

Swift Arrow's first winter away from home passed quickly. He often joined the braves in hunting animals for food. He became experienced with use of the bow and arrow and the gun, and Big Wolf taught him to recognize animal tracks and caves that animals lived in. He taught George to recognize bruised leaves or slight scrapes on tree trunks as signs of animals nearby. The weather was mild that winter and the snow light. This allowed George to spend much time practicing in the oval arena. Probably to help build his confidence, the teacher first drilled George on running, a sport that he soon mastered. Within a few months George learned to outdistance the Indian boys of his own age and many of the older ones. Now the boys looked at him with more respect. And still the teacher continued to drill him at wrestling. Some days it rained, but the teacher did not let up. At evening George would emerge from the arena black with mud. Mud caked his hair and his ears, and even his mouth tasted of mud. But George learned that winter to be a champion wrestler.

Nobody felt more pleased about George's new success than Big Wolf. He regarded the boy proudly, and during council with the warriors often boasted of George's achievements.

"Swift Arrow has become as true an Indian as any of us in the village," Big Wolf would say. "Soon he will be the bravest and the strongest. Already his muscles bulge as hard as steel."

And it was true. George had gathered much new strength during the winter. And on the long marches and hunting trips he learned to endure cold and hunger as well as any Indian. But what Big Wolf did not realize was that George had not become a true Indian at all. He acted like one publicly. But privately his thoughts strayed to his home and his parents. He thought longingly of the good food Ma cooked. And he remembered the pretty fairness of his sister Zella and Robert's sister Becky. How they contrasted to the stern, bronze maidens of the Indian village! Would he ever see them again? Every day now George prayed that God would help him find his way back home. He had lost all hope that Pa and the other settlers could ever track him down in this wilderness. But he still felt sure God would somehow lead him back to them.

Spring arrived, and George rejoiced to see tender buds bursting from the brown tree branches. He and his friends raced their ponies along the wooded paths and through fields decorated with dainty wild flowers, yellow, orange, and purple. They passed men making new canoes and women planting the fields with corn and vegetables. George thought it strange to see the women working in the fields, but he knew that was the Indian custom.

"Pa's probably planting his fields now too," George thought. "And I ought to be there to help him. Well, someday I'll be there. Just wait!"

George made a new friend that spring, a tall, muscular Indian boy named White Rabbit. George judged the boy to be about his own age. They spent many hours together in the fields and woods, and had fun wrestling and racing each other in the arena. First one would win, then the other. Of all the Indian boys George had met, White Rabbit seemed the kindest and most understanding.

But it was only to his little sister Ewanah that George revealed the true secrets of his heart. When he felt sad and lonely, he would go to her and talk about the home and family he missed so much.

"You would like it, Ewanah. I know you would. The homes are

made from logs. They are always dry, and the wind does not blow in. Ma and Pa sleep on a soft bed, and the rest of us—."

"A bed? What is a bed?" Ewanah would interrupt.

"A bed? Why it has something called a mattress that rests off the ground on top of wooden boards. The mattress is soft and stuffed with feathers from geese and ducks. And people lie down on the mattress to sleep."

Ewanah would look puzzled, but nod her little head as though she understood.

"Would you not like to live in such a warm house, Ewanah?"

"Oh, no, Swift Arrow! I am an Indian. I would die if I had to live in such a way."

Then George would tell her about the good food Ma cooked.

"She makes something called bread. It is made by grinding wheat grain as the squaws grind the grain of corn. Ma mixes it up real good and then puts it into long, narrow pans. When the bread is baked it is the same shape as the pan. It has a hard crust on the outside and soft brown dough on the inside."

Ewanah giggled. "I would like to eat such food," she whispered. "Do you think you could make some?"

"No, I am sure I could not," George answered indignantly. "Ma and my sisters did all the cooking. Cooking's for women, not men!"

"How do women have time to make such food, Swift Arrow? Do they not hoe the fields and plant the corn?"

"No. That work is left to the men who are stronger. The women keep busy all day with their cooking and other jobs like weaving carpets and cloth, and knitting."

"Knitting?" Ewanah looked puzzled again.

"Sure, knitting! The women take the wool from the back of sheep and spin it into string. Then they take long needles and sort of loop the string all together so that it is smooth and warm and can be made into warm coverings for the feet and hands and neck."

Ewanah shrugged her shoulders. "Well, I do not know what these words 'needle' and 'string' mean. But I am sure it must be just as you say, Swift Arrow."

Then she would playfully pull at his dark hair, and he would chase her until they both fell down laughing. Though Ewanah did not understand all that George told her about his home, she did understand one thing very clearly. She knew that she must never breathe a word of the things he told her to Big Wolf or any of the other Indians. If they knew that he still thought longingly of home, they would probably beat him or maybe even kill him.

One day when George was hiking with Big Wolf through the woods, his curiosity got the best of him. More than anything he wanted to know if Ma and Pa had been killed in the Indian raid or if they still lived. Surely Big Wolf could tell him that much! As the two sat down to rest on a log, George finally plucked up the nerve to blurt his question.

"Honored Father, will you please give me the answer to one question that keeps me sad wondering?"

The chief's coal black eyes bored into him, but George hurried on. "The day I was taken from my home, I saw smoke coming through the windows of my house. Were my father and mother killed that day? And what about Robert, the friend that was taken with me?"

Big Wolf fixed George with a fierce look that seemed to freeze him to the log. George wanted to run, but his legs would not move. For a long time the chief continued to stare at George with a look of pure fury. Finally George could take it no longer, and tripping backward over the log, scurried frantically into the woods. Would the chief kill him for his daring questions?

"Get back here!" Big Wolf roared, and the command stopped

George in his tracks. He slowly returned and sat on the log. Big Wolf seized George by the shoulders and shook him like Ewanah's dog shook the long-nosed rats he caught nibbling in the food-storage place.

"I am your father!" Big Wolf cried, as he continued to shake the terrified George. "I am your father, and you have no mother!" Then Big Wolf stopped shaking George, and the Indian suddenly looked very tired.

"Swift Arrow, you are not a prisoner here," he said in a gentler voice. "You are with your own people now. Nobody so strong, and brave, and clever as you, was born to be a paleface! You may have been born among the palefaces, but you were born to be an Indian. You are with your own people now, and you must forget the other days when you were a weak papoose. How dare you think of that friend of yours who was a sickly rabbit, weaker than a squaw! Forget him! And forget that other life. Never again speak to me of that which is not worth re-membering. You will be told what you are to know."

Big Wolf rose abruptly from the log and strode back toward the vil-lage. George followed, careful to keep a safe distance behind.

"He may think he can make me forget my ma and pa, but he can't!" George thought stubbornly, "He can't tell what's going on inside my head. Someday I'll show him!"

For several days Big Wolf ignored George. But gradually his heart began to melt. As he watched George play with the other Indian boys and follow the many Indian customs, he must have decided that George really was becoming a good Indian after all. He and George resumed their hunting and hiking together, and occasionally Big Wolf even discussed some of the business of governing the village with George. George listened eagerly and tried hard to please this chief who had obvi-ously come to love him as a son.

One of George's greatest ordeals was learning to swim. Water had frightened him ever since the time he almost drowned when he was about two or three years old. George watched the Indian boys and decided they could swim almost as well as the fish in the lake. But no matter how much time they spent showing George just the right motions to make in the water, George could not swim. Every time he lifted his feet from the lake bottom, his head would sink under water and he'd cough and sputter, thinking he would drown for sure.

George's failure to swim became a great worry to Big Wolf. Every Indian boy must swim. Sometimes the ability to swim even saved their lives. The chief often reproached George about swimming and accused him of not trying hard enough. One day the chief called George to him.

"Come, Swift Arrow. Today we will take a canoe onto the lake and go fishing."

George had often gone fishing on the lake with Big Wolf, so he expected nothing unusual. Instead, he gladly ran for their fishing lines and a little pot of bait and was opposite Big Wolf in the canoe within minutes. Usually George did the paddling on such fishing trips. But today Big Wolf surprised him by reaching for the paddle himself. The slender prow of the light canoe cut swiftly through the deep blue water as the chief's powerful arms dipped and pulled the paddle. Not until they had gone about a hundred yards from shore did he stop.

"What do you think we'll catch today?" George asked eagerly.

Big Wolf gave him an amused look. "Today we will see a big fish swim."

This answer puzzled George. Hadn't he seen many big fish swim? What he wanted was to catch a big fish!

"Oh, well, who can know what the chief is thinking?" George said to himself. "Anyway, it's too beautiful a day to worry."

After a few minutes of quiet fishing, the chief began struggling with his line. "Big fish! Big fish!" he exclaimed.

87

"So soon?" George asked, and he turned around to watch the chief land his fish. As he turned, a powerful shove and lift from behind sent George spinning into the deep lake.

"Help! Help!" George cried, swallowing big gulps of water as he opened his mouth. He reached frantically for the canoe, but it was not there. "Help! Help!" George thrashed and kicked as he felt himself sinking under the water. Where was the chief? Why did he not help? The chief knew he couldn't swim!

George's head bobbed to the surface, and what he saw made him regain his senses. The chief was paddling away, apparently not at all concerned about George's cries. The Indian did not even look back to see how he made out.

"Why, he did it purposely!" George thought between sputtering gasps for breath. "He purposely pushed me into the water so I'd have to swim." Then George realized that he was already keeping afloat. He had unconsciously begun moving his arms and legs as the boys had told him to do so many times before. But this time it worked. Now, what else had they said about swimming? He tried to remember their careful instructions, and before long he found himself slowly moving through the water toward shore. He cupped the palms of his hands and pushed down on the water as though he wanted to push it under him. Then he kicked his feet in time with the movements of his arms.

"I'm swimming! I'm swimming!" he kept repeating to himself. He looked toward Big Wolf's canoe and saw that the chief had stopped but was carefully ignoring his struggling son.

"I guess he'd rather have me drown than have me continue such a babyish habit as being scared of the water."

Now he began lifting his arms high over his head before putting them into the water, and he discovered that the more powerful thrusts made him move faster. He turned his head from side to side to take big breaths and kicked harder with his feet. The shore seemed to come closer and closer. Then he noticed a large group of boys gathered on the shore. They were waving their hands and shouting something.

"Swift Arrow swims! Swift Arrow swims!" he heard them call.

When he reached shallow water, he put down his feet and walked toward the shore. As the boys cheered, George began cheering, too. He shouted with the rest of them and laughed when a few broke into a brief Indian war dance. George looked back at the lake and saw that Big Wolf had begun paddling toward shore. When the chief came out of the water, he pulled the canoe onto dry ground and walked away without saying a word. But he had a pleasant twinkle in his dark eyes, and George knew he felt pleased.

As the spring days passed to summer, George spent much time in the water. He learned to tread water, float, dive, and swim underwater. By the beginning of winter he was winning not only many land races but water races as well.

The first few winters George spent at the Indian village passed quickly for him because there were so many new things to learn. But by the time he was about fifteen, he began to dread winter. The new experiences had grown old and no longer fascinated him. The cold winds and snow made it impossible to wrestle in the arena or practice running and jumping. Much of the lake lay frozen, so of course he couldn't swim. Snowdrifts piled too high in the woods to risk riding Neko very far. But, George noticed, the lack of something to do didn't seem to bother the other young braves. In fact, they welcomed the chance to sleep or rest lazily on piles of skins while they watched the squaws cook, make pottery, or sew skins together for clothes.

The Indians must have thought it queer when they saw George come in from the forest carrying huge loads of firewood for the squaws. Big Wolf looked questioningly at him, and finally White Rabbit called

George aside and told him not to bother himself with squaws' work.

"So now what can I do with myself?" George wondered silently. Then he remembered something. Robert's sister Becky had had a playhouse back in Germantown, and how the girls had loved to play in it! It had been made big enough for the girls to walk around in; some of the ladies furnished old dishes and a few kettles, and Mrs. Stewart had even made some curtains for the windows.

"Why not make a playhouse for Ewanah?" George thought. "She'd love it! And the other little girls would flock to it too."

George could hardly wait to begin. First he searched in the snowy woods for logs of just the right thickness. He even took his hatchet and chopped down a few young trees. Then he hauled the logs to a clear area near Ewanah's wigwam and began the slow task of splitting them.

"What are you doing, Swift Arrow?" Ewanah asked the day he deposited the logs in the clearing.

George just smiled.

"Please, Swift Arrow. Tell me what you are doing!"

"It is a surprise."

"A surprise for me?"

"Yes, for you."

"Will I like it?"

"I hope so."

"Oh, please tell me what it is!"

But George refused to tell and just continued his work.

Every day Ewanah came to watch as George notched logs and fitted them together. He built the little house as he remembered his father had built their cabin in the settlement. What he could not remember, he improvised. In just a few days the cabin began to take shape, and Ewanah guessed what he was building.

"It looks like the log houses that you say your people live in, Swift

Arrow. Is that what you are building?"

"It is a little house like the big houses of my people. When I have finished building it, you can play inside with your friends."

Ewanah jumped up and down and cried little cries of delight.

"Oh, Swift Arrow, you are the most wonderful of all the brothers in the village! When will it be finished? You must hurry before the snows become too deep for you to work outside."

"If you're in such a hurry, then you can just help me."

"Can I really? What can I do?"

George showed Ewanah how to mix mud and push it into the cracks between the logs just as he had done for his father years before.

"The mud will keep out the snow and cold winds. If you work carefully your little house will be the warmest place in the whole village."

For the next few days Ewanah's slender legs climbed all over the cabin, as she carefully poked mud into the cracks. When George finished the outside, he began eagerly on the inside. First he made a fireplace of sticks and clay. Then with his hatchet and knife he fashioned a small table and two stools, fitting their parts together with pins as Pa had done with the ones he made for Ma. He pegged crude shelves on both sides of the fireplace.

Because the affairs of government had kept the chief especially busy that winter, George saw little of him. But he sometimes wondered uncomfortably just how Big Wolf would react to having his precious daughter play in a paleface cabin. Would he be angry? One morning as George sat inside the little house smoothing logs for the floor, he looked out the door to see Big Wolf walking toward him. George hastily dropped his tools and stepped outside to meet the chief.

"It is good to see you, honored Father. You have been working too hard lately."

"I see that you, too, have been working hard. Every morning I look

91

and I see the little house looks more nearly finished."

Big Wolf did not smile as he spoke, and his eyes seemed to bore holes through George as they always did when he was angry. Just then Ewanah stepped out from her wigwam. Seeing her, the chief's look softened.

"Oh, Father, do you see the beautiful playhouse my brother has built for me? Is it not wonderful? And will I not have great fun playing inside? Come inside and see the table and stools and the fireplace that Swift Arrow has made."

Big Wolf did as she asked and nodded his head in approval at the furniture. He ran his hand over the smooth tabletop and carefully examined the fireplace.

"Now winter will not be so tiresome for me, Father. I can play with my friends in my own house. And is it not very warm inside?"

It seemed that Big Wolf could not be angry about the paleface house when his little daughter felt so delighted with it.

"It is good that your brother has made this house for you. Be careful when you play that you do not hurt yourself," the chief said. When he walked outside, the curious squaws noted that he was smiling.

Now that the house had the blessing of the chief, it seemed that every squaw in the village wanted to see inside. Most of them had never seen a paleface house. Every day old wrinkled grandmothers and pretty young maidens came to poke their heads through the doorway and watch George finish the floor. When at last he had finished, squaws began leaving little gifts inside for Ewanah. One brought a pair of brightly painted pots. Another brought an old kettle, which George hung over the fireplace. Still another set a pretty china sugar bowl on the table. Painted brown flowers decorated its sides, and a lid sat on top. George knew that it must be a prize brought by some raiding party. Finally Ewanah's own old grandmother came with a fluffy brown bearskin and laid it proudly before the fireplace.

Now that George had completed the house, he began working on another project. Every evening Ewanah saw him carving a small piece of wood. First he worked it into a round shape. Then he began notching and cutting. He called Ewanah to sit down before him and spent several minutes studying her face. When next she came back she discovered that he had fashioned a little wooden head that looked a great deal like her. Next he cut some doeskin from one of the skins he slept on, borrowed a bone needle and tough thread from the old squaw, and began sewing. When he finished the sewing, he held up a crudely shaped body. He fastened arms and legs to it with leather thongs so that they moved.

When he had finished fastening the head to the body, George discovered to his surprise that the old squaw had been working, too. She smiled a toothless grin and handed him a delicate beaded dress and tiny moccasins.

"Yes, this is just what we need!" George exclaimed gratefully. He quickly slipped the dress over the head, and the squaw nodded her approval. When Ewanah saw the finished toy, she cried for joy.

"Oh, a baby! A little, wooden papoose for me to play with!"

George laughed. "My sister at home used to call these 'dolls,' and my grandfather in Germantown called them 'poppets.' So, Ewanah, I have made you a poppet."

The squaw made a papoose board for Ewanah, and she carried the doll on her back everywhere she went about the village. At first the other squaws looked at the doll suspiciously. Perhaps they thought it was a real baby. But when they at last realized it was a little toy, they began to wish their girls had one to play with. Thus George kept himself busy many of those cold winter days making poppets for little Indian maidens.

*George sat with the village medicine men to gather
a knowledge of medicine. They taught him to select
and prepare certain herbs and plants good for sicknesses.*

Chapter 12

Trial by Knives

George raced Neko through a grassy field and up the steep slope of a hill. Then he stopped to enjoy the beauty of the spring afternoon. Below to the left shimmered the great lake, blue and rippling in the sunlight. Far to the right lay the Indian village. He had lived in that village for almost ten years now. He smiled as he remembered the experiences of the first year. The pawing he had taken from the squaws as they inspected the first paleface boy they had ever seen. The ordeal he had faced in the oval arena—learning to wrestle and then that first race. Well, all that lay behind him. Nobody in the village could outrun, outwrestle, or outswim him now. And the Indians accepted him as one of themselves. He ate, slept, talked, worked, and played like an Indian. And because of the brown stain he had to paint on his body every few months, he looked like an Indian too. Already his shoulders had grown broad and muscular. And he stood a full six feet tall.

"But I am not an Indian!" George said fiercely to himself now. "I am not a redskin! And if I'm ever going to return to the kind of life I want to live, a nice, peaceful life in a quiet settlement, I'd best do something about it fast."

Big Wolf had shown signs of age the last few years. His life had been hard and full of responsibilities that seemed to have aged him faster than normal. It was common talk throughout the tribe that Big Wolf would choose his son, Swift Arrow, as new chief when he died. George knew that if he were ever to escape, it would have to be before any official announcement from Big Wolf. But how? Even now the chief kept a fairly close watch on him. And George still did not know how many days' journey the Indian village lay from his home settlement. Nor did he know whether Ma and Pa still lived.

As George sat thinking, he heard the pounding rhythm of horse's hooves coming near. Turning, he saw White Rabbit galloping up the hill.

"Where have you been?" White Rabbit called as soon as he was in yelling distance. "I have looked all over for you. The chief, your father, wants to see you. He sent me to find you and bring you to him."

This news made George feel uneasy. What could Big Wolf want that was too important to wait until supper time?

"Did he mention why he wants me?" George asked.

"No. He just said to find you."

Reaching the wigwam he had long shared with the chief, George found Big Wolf propped up on a pile of soft skins with blankets behind him. The chief was fully dressed in his usual clothes, but George felt surprised to see how old and tired he looked. "How is it that he has grown old before my eyes without my noticing it," he thought? The chief had been kind to George, and the boy had developed a strong affection for him. Big Wolf pointed to a place on the floor, and George sat down.

"My son, you can see that my body has grown weak," Big Wolf began. "I have been sick for many moons. Before many more moons pass I will not be with you to lead my people."

George started to protest, but the chief put up his hand for silence. "Do not feel sad. I do not fear leaving you, for I know I leave the tribe in good hands. You are brave, strong, and wise. I have trained you to endure much and to be fearless in the face of danger. To you will fall the responsibility of leading this people. You will be chief when I have

96

passed over to a better hunting ground."

George had been expecting this from Big Wolf, but now that the time had come, he scarcely knew what to say. When he finally did speak, he chose his words carefully.

"There is no need to speak of such matters, honored one. For your people love you and will take care of you so that your life shall last many more years. We are your children. We do not like to hear you say you will not longer lead us."

"All men must die!" the chief said, with some of his old fierceness. "And it is with their children that they must trust the next generation. You will take the load from my shoulders when I am gone."

"I am honored that you choose me for this," George said. "But there is no need for us to speak of it now. You will have many more years in which to enjoy the love of your people." So saying, George backed from the presence of the chief into the bright sunshine.

"The time has grown later than I thought," he said to himself as he walked slowly through the village.

George waited the next day for a chance to catch his sister Ewanah alone. He found her late in the morning sitting near her wigwam sewing colorful beads onto a headband.

"How pretty she has become," George thought. "So slender and graceful! Never have I seen a more beautiful girl."

Ewanah smiled when she saw him coming.

"My brother," she said, "it has been many days since I have talked with you. You keep yourself too busy."

"Then come with me now, Ewanah. We'll take a ride together."

A worried look clouded George's handsome face as the two rode silently over the familiar trails. Ewanah was first to speak.

"Something important is on your mind, Swift Arrow. What is it?"

"I am greatly troubled, little sister. As you know, our father plans to make me chief soon. When he does so, it will be almost impossible for me to carry out the plans I used to speak to you about."

"Plans? What plans?"

"Why, the plans for me to leave this village and return home to the settlement of my real parents."

"Oh, Swift Arrow! After all the years do you still remember that old home? Why do you not be happy with the honor that will be given you here? You are to become leader of a mighty nation of people."

"Ewanah, you have long known my feelings. Real living means a clean home, neat clothing, busy schools, quiet churches, and the love of your family. That is the way my people taught me as a boy. I cannot be happy with this uncertain life, never sure of enough food, always depending on the hunt and the small gardens of the squaws. And many of our people here are dirty and lazy. But worst of all, Ewanah, as chief of these people I would be forced to lead them on raids and help them steal and kill. I could never do that! Those we would rob would be people of my own blood. You know that it is impossible."

To no Indian other than Ewanah would George have dared speak such words. Yet this gentle girl always seemed to understand and almost agree.

"I can see what you mean. You are still too much of a paleface to be happy with the Indian life. You must have enjoyed your paleface life, for you still remember it though you were so little when you came here."

"If you could know my good mother and father, Ewanah, you would know the reason. They enjoyed life, and they taught us to enjoy life too."

"I can see that you must go, though it will make Big Wolf very sad, and a light will also go from my life. When the time comes, I will help you. You can depend on that. But until then, we must keep it secret between us."

George and Ewanah continued to ride in silence, enjoying what they expected to be one of their last rides together. After a time, Ewanah spoke again.

"Swift Arrow, I, too, have a favor to ask. Our father may soon decide to give me in marriage to one of the braves. When that time comes, he may speak to you for counsel. If he does, will you—will you—"

Ewanah suddenly seemed too shy to continue. George grinned.

"Ha! I know what you are going to say, before you say it. You want me to mention the name of White Rabbit as a husband for you. Is that not right?"

"Yes, my brother. You have read my heart."

"Very well, if the opportunity comes to me, I shall speak up loudly in behalf of White Rabbit."

Ewanah smiled happily.

"I'm sure he will make you a good husband," George said. "And because he is your husband, Big Wolf will make him chief when I go. I feel certain that White Rabbit could make a mighty chief and bring honor upon this tribe."

So far George had passed every test of the Indians, often doing far better than the Indian boys. The teachers taught him their knowledge of astronomy, woodcraft, and trailing. From the skies, tree bark, moss, and animal skins, George had learned to detect signs of hot or cold weather. From the village medicine man he had gathered a knowledge of medicine that every chief must know. The medicine man showed him how to select from the forests and fields certain herbs, plants, roots, and barks that could be used for medicine. He taught George the use of the medicines and how to prepare them. Together they pounded ointments for treating wounds. George learned what to do for fevers, chills, or sickness of the heart and lungs.

But George knew that soon he would be expected to pass the most difficult test of all. This test was an initiation ceremony marking passage from Indian boyhood to manhood. Failing it meant great dishonor. About fifty boys would participate.

The test had been scheduled to take place early that spring, and George watched the preparations for several weeks before. Hunters came back from the forests with large catches of deer, bear, and wild turkey. Squaws worked far into the nights cleaning meat from the hides. Big Wolf directed the braves to make shelters for the large numbers of neighboring Indians expected to come. He told George to help other braves get bark from the forests to be used on the outside of the shelters.

As George worked, he shuddered to think of what lay ahead. This test was a true game of hazard. He had seen it once before soon after coming to the village. Two lines of warriors faced each other. Each held a sharp knife in his outstretched hand, but he could bend his arm only at the elbow. First the warriors bent their elbows to hold the knives straight up, then together in time to the measured rhythm of the drums, they let their arms fall straight out in a slashing motion. They brought them up again and then let them fall. About two feet separated the lines when the warriors held the knives out straight. And along this long, narrow path the young men who hoped to be accepted as braves, eligible for marriage and ready for war, must all run. Yes, George remembered the ceremony well because he had felt so terrified the first time he saw it. Many of the young men had been so badly slashed by the blades that they had lost their nerve halfway through. He could still see them as they fell bleeding to the ground. Others became hooked on the knives again and again but continued steadily, only to fall just a few yards from the finish. Many of those who did complete the course had to be carried away from the finish line, so great were their wounds. Few indeed managed to run a straight enough course to escape without serious, gaping wounds.

"What shame I will bring to Big Wolf if I fall before the finish," George thought. "For Big Wolf's sake at least I must come through the ordeal whole and well, without any serious wounds. But how? What can I do to prepare myself?"

Then George thought of an idea. He waited until the men had gathered enough bark. As soon as they headed back toward the village, he ran deeper into the forest. When he came to a small clearing, he took up a stick and drew a long, straight line. Then he practiced running along the line, careful not to move his shoulders and holding his arms completely still. He stayed in the woods for several hours. Then, noticing that the sun had set, he decided he had practiced enough for one day.

"I'll return here again tomorrow," he told himself as he started back toward the village. "I must be able to run without moving my body from side to side. And I must be able to run swiftly so that not many knives will slash at me."

After practice the next morning, George felt more confident. "I am ready," he thought. "Tomorrow I will not be afraid. Big Wolf will be proud of his son."

Long before George reached the village borders, he caught the aroma of meat cooking. In the village he found hundreds of huge pots bubbling full of Indian stew. The pots hung over open fires, and squaws stirred the stew with long paddles. Sides of deer meat roasted on spits over other fires. Young village girls spelled one another at turning the spits. George noticed many strange faces throughout the village. Visitors from brother tribes had already begun arriving.

And George saw to his dismay that the warriors who would participate in tomorrow's initiation ceremony had already begun practicing with their knives. They had been arranged in two lines facing each other, just as George remembered from the time before. As he moved closer to watch, he saw that all the warriors held their arms out straight, and inspectors walked between the two rows measuring arms with a pole. Occasionally an inspector sent one warrior away and called another to take his place. Only warriors with arms of the correct length could participate, for the path between them must be uniform in width all along the line. Now an inspector pointed his finger at several Indians who stood nearby holding drums. Immediately they began beating the drums in rhythm. At another signal from the inspector, the two lines of warriors bent their elbows, bringing up the knives. Then all together they straightened their arms so the knives pointed toward the center. Up and down went their arms, the knives gleaming and flashing in the sunlight. While they all tried to move their arms at the same time, some had difficulty. George watched for about fifteen minutes. Then he went to help the men finish the shelters for their visitors. When he returned several hours later, the warriors were still practicing. But now their timing seemed perfect. All the arms moved as if from one body. George guessed that the inspectors had replaced any warriors who could not keep correct time with others who were more coordinated.

George decided to spend the remaining few hours of daylight practicing in the woods. A crowd had gathered to watch the two lines of warriors. He shouldered his way past an old chief whom he didn't recognize. The chief leaned toward one of his braves to say something, but the brave must have been slightly hard of hearing, for the chief spoke loudly.

"Who is this brave who walks so proudly?" the chief asked.

"I hear that he is the son of Big Wolf," the Indian answered.

"The son of Big Wolf? Is not Big Wolf's son a papoose taken from the paleface?"

"Many years ago. But his people say the boy's heart now beats with the courage of an Indian. He is one of us."

The old chief grunted, but George was too far away by now to be sure what he said. He thought it sounded like, "We will see tomorrow!"

"Well, and I'll show him, too," George thought defiantly as he ran toward his clearing in the woods.

That night the Indians played games in the moonlight. When they tired of the games, a great campfire was built, and they sat down to enjoy the stories of the old warriors. They told of past glories, long years before the paleface had come to destroy their hunting grounds. Some told tales of the spirits they worshiped. Younger men boasted proudly of their tribes' bravery against present enemies, both Indian and paleface. George listened but kept silent. He fumed inside as he heard stories of treachery against his own people. When the storytellers grew quiet and the drums began to beat, George felt almost relieved. Through the years he had become used to the wild ceremonial dances. But he slipped away into the darkness. Though he had grown used to them, George still did not enjoy the dances.

"I'd much rather be singing with my family around a cozy fire in a cabin's stone fireplace."

Visitors and villagers alike passed the next morning in more games and wrestling and racing events. George did not participate, because he wanted to be fresh for the big ceremony everybody impatiently waited for. It was not to begin until mid-afternoon, after the heat of the day had passed. About an hour before the appointed time, people began to gather in the oval arena where the ceremony would take place. Everyone from wrinkled old squaw to proud chief was anxious to get a good place to sit, preferably a place on the hill in order to be in the best position to see. George also walked to the arena and joined the other young men who would take the test. They all had the same question: Will I pass or fail? If they failed, they could only wait in shame until the next initiation when they could try again.

Now the warriors took their places in the two long lines. The waiting crowd was a buzz of excitement. Drums beat slowly, then faster and faster. Inspectors lined up the young men in order of their appearance in the test. George discovered unhappily that he would be the center of attraction. Because he was son of Big Wolf, and a former paleface at that, the people felt particularly eager to see him perform. Thus he would run last in the contest that the best might be saved until last.

As the crowd of hundreds watched, two lines of evenly matched warriors let their arms fall out straight, their sharp knives flashing. They began a steady slashing motion in time to the drumbeats. The knives had been made razor sharp on pumice stone. No emotion showed on the faces of the boys who waited to run between the two lines. If they felt scared, they did not show it. Nor did the first one show it if he felt reluctant to begin. For he moved calmly between the lines of warriors, hesitating slightly when a blade gashed his arm, and stumbling when the knives caught him again, one in each shoulder, as he neared the finish. But he ran it well, and the people cheered. Thus the young man who had begun the ordeal as a boy came out a brave. Now the crowd turned its attention eagerly to the second boy. He did not do as well. His wounds were more severe, but he managed to stagger through the last of the warriors. The third boy fell two-thirds of the way through. The crowd roared their disapproval, and the unfortunate boy was carried away to have his wounds dressed. As the boys continued to run, most managed to reach the finish, though just barely, and many with

ugly, gaping gashes across their arms, shoulders, and backs. A few
had even been slashed in the head. Of those who fell before the finish,
many were hauled away unconscious.

After the third or fourth runner had fallen, George stopped watching. It seemed that the more times he saw the knives flash against
the boys' flesh, leaving ugly, bleeding cuts, the more his courage faded. Then the last of his companions disappeared through the rows of
slashing knives, and George heard his own name called.

"Swift Arrow, son of Big Wolf."

"I must keep calm," George reminded himself as he walked slowly to the first set of warriors. "I must ignore the knives and warriors
and run swiftly as I did in the woods."

George held his head high, took a deep breath, and sprinted down
the narrow path. Knives flashed on both sides of him, but to his surprise he did not feel worried. He felt strong, and this race seemed
scarcely different from the ones he had practiced running in the
woods. Once he felt a sharp sting as a knife scratched at his shoulder,
but he had known much worse pain than that. Again, halfway through
the course another knife caught the same shoulder, but he didn't even
feel it. Several more times the knives scratched and scraped his skin;
but when George emerged from the end of the course, he knew only
that a tremendous cheer louder than any he had ever heard greeted his
ears. He had run swiftly through the two lines, never hesitating and
receiving only slight wounds. Seldom did the Indians get to see such
a fine performance.

"Why, they're cheering for me," George thought, "and for Big
Wolf!" Though he felt more pleased than he had ever felt, he made
certain that his pleasure did not show. Like a good Indian, he must
keep his face a mask of unconcern. But then when his friends crowded
around him, he could not help but join in their laughter and good hu-

mor. The best congratulations of all came from Big Wolf.

"Today is the proudest day of my life. You have proved yourself a true Indian and a good son. And have proved me right in choosing you for my son."

Chapter 13

A Bride for a Prize

George hurried toward his wigwam after supper. Today had been an exciting day. The visiting Indians treated him with new respect after his performance during the initiation ceremony. Even the chiefs had taken trouble to seek his friendship. During supper they told him to sit at the honored place to the right of Big Wolf. But when they had eaten the meal, George noticed braves building a huge bonfire in the arena. Figuring they were preparing for more dancing and storytelling that night, he decided to return to his wigwam. He had grown tired of the beating drums, and he did not enjoy the stories.

Now the brave Running Water, a friend of George's, interrupted his thinking. He said something that George did not understand.

"What is this you say, my friend?" George asked.

"I say that tonight should prove interesting. Don't you agree?"

"Interesting? Why interesting?" George said. "I grow weary of the old warriors' tales."

"Tales? Why surely you know that tonight we will hear no tales. Tonight is the night we shall receive our brides."

George's eyes flashed angrily. "Why have I not been told of this before?"

"Ha! I am sure I do not know. Perhaps Big Wolf wanted to surprise you. Each of the braves who passed the ceremony today shall be given a bride."

"But I do not want a bride," George said.

"You are joking, Swift Arrow. We are all anxious to see which of the maidens will be given to us. Considered most beautiful of all is your own sister, Ewanah. Lucky is the brave who carries her away as his prize."

George turned back toward the arena. He knew he would be expected to attend this ceremony. As the crowd gathered, he glanced occasionally at Ewanah. He had to agree that she did look lovely. Dressed in white doeskin that set off well her proud, dark beauty, she held her head high and kept her eyes fixed straight ahead. Her dress was fringed at the bottom and embroidered with colorful beads. Strings of beads had been gathered into the long braids that reached to her hips, and a beaded headband wound around her forehead. Ewanah looked unconcerned, but George knew how anxious she must really feel. Did she not want more than anything else to become the squaw of White Rabbit? George hoped fervently that his beautiful young sister might get her wish.

Now Big Wolf rose to speak, and the crowd waited respectfully. His voice sounded weak, but he spoke firmly and without hesitation.

"Many years ago I took a beautiful young bride as many of our braves will do tonight. We passed several moons of great happiness, but the time came when an illness carried her away. She went home to the Great Spirit, but not without leaving a little girl child to comfort me. This child became the light of my life, but I perceived that I needed a son. And then the Great Spirit took pity upon me and sent a son, a fine, strong son who has become the bravest of the brave, the strongest of the strong. He is the strength of my heart as my body grows weak from sickness."

The crowd watched as Big Wolf called for Ewanah and Swift Arrow to join him. They took their places, one on each side of the chief. Ewanah stood erect, but turned her eyes modestly to the ground.

George, on the other hand, folded his arms across his powerful chest and gazed boldly though respectfully into the crowd. Big Wolf continued his speech.

"What better union could be made than the marriage of my beautiful daughter left me by my beloved wife and my strong son sent me by the Great Spirit? Thus let it be known that at such a season as my daughter, Ewanah, becomes old enough to be taken as a bride, she shall be received by my son, Swift Arrow. I feel a perfect trust in him. He has been victor in all contests with other braves, and you saw his great performance in today's ceremony. It is with him that I shall leave my trust when I go to the Great Spirit. He shall become your leader, a wise, strong, good leader whom you will love and respect."

Then Big Wolf told his son and daughter to take their places side by side by the fire, and the chief proceeded to announce the betrothal of other braves. But George, feeling confused and unhappy, did not hear anything more. Ewanah, too, sat silent and unseeing.

"This cannot be," George thought. "I must get away from here before Big Wolf dies, or it will be too late. But how?"

George knew that if he disappeared, the best warriors would be sent to bring him back. And his disappearance would be considered the act of a coward, reason enough for death according to Indian thinking. "No, I must not act hastily," George told himself. "I must move cautiously, planning everything."

A few days later Ewanah asked George to join her for a ride through the woods. It was the first time they had been alone since the night of the betrothals. As soon as they reached the first of the familiar forest paths, Ewanah blurted what she had on her mind.

"I can tell that you do not want me for your squaw, Swift Arrow." George remained silent for a moment.

"You are my sister. It is neither the custom of my people nor of

109

your people for brother to marry sister."

"You are right. And only because our father knows that we are not really brother and sister, can he do this. Otherwise the people would not let him. But what Father could never understand is that while I love you as a brother I could never love you as I love White Rabbit. Somehow I must become the squaw of White Rabbit."

George felt relieved. Now, at least, he knew Ewanah would not feel hurt that he rejected her for his squaw.

"There is only one thing to do, my sister. I must leave this village and return to my people."

Ewanah let out a little gasp of surprise.

"But, Swift Arrow, we have talked of this before! And never can we find a way for you to go. I am afraid it is useless even to hope that you will ever find happiness among your own people."

"No, Ewanah. That is not true. I believe that my God will some-day answer my prayer to Him. Many times I pray that He will show me the way to leave here. Now I think that perhaps He has waited until such a time as now, when I am older and stronger and understand the ways of the forest. I probably could not have survived in the woods if I had tried escaping when I was still a child. Now I am a man."

Ewanah smiled. "Perhaps you are right. If you still hope, then so will I. And I will try to help you. I just wish there were some other way, for I shall miss you greatly."

"There is no other way," George said quietly.

In the winter that followed George became a great help to the chief. Together they considered plans to increase the village pros-perity, and it was George who suggested in council meeting that the squaws be directed to plant larger areas of land in corn, squash, and beans. George helped Big Wolf in other ways. He dug roots and herbs from under the snow in the forest and pounded them and mixed them into strong medicines. Given to the chief, the medicines seemed to help him, and by spring he was walking about the village, though not so firmly as he once had.

One day that spring Big Wolf suggested that it was about time for George to marry Ewanah.

"I feel so much better now that it seems I will live to see my children married after all. The marriage must be soon, before the winter winds bring sickness again. Perhaps if the marriage is soon I shall even live to see my first grandchild."

George felt dismayed at Big Wolf's urgency. But he didn't know what to say. It was Ewanah who came to the rescue.

"Oh, no, Father, I cannot marry yet. I am not wise enough to become the wife of a chief. We must wait until I learn more things from the old women."

Big Wolf shook his head angrily. But when Ewanah ran to him and knelt at his feet, crying, "Please, Father, give me the time I need to become a good wife," he seemed powerless to refuse her.

"Very well. We will wait yet a little while."

Another year passed. Big Wolf spent the winter in much pain, often feeling cross and impatient. When nature showed signs of spring, he sent for George.

"I have set the time for your wedding feast, my son. Your maid still insists on more time, but she does not know her mind. She has had more than enough time to get ready. You shall be married during the next moon."

As news of the marriage spread throughout the village, people began to prepare for the feast. Hunters brought back several young does, and the squaws set to work immediately curing the hides which would be used for Ewanah's wedding dress. Only the softest and whitest of hides would have this honor. The squaws took equal care in preparing hides for George's clothing. After all, would he not soon become their chief?

It seemed that the whole village rejoiced with the good news of the long-awaited wedding. Everyone, that is, except the two most concerned. Now that their wedding day drew near, Ewanah and Swift Arrow grew fearful. Though they were seldom allowed to be alone together, they were quick to take advantage of what opportunities did come. Occasionally they slipped away into the forests, and the village elders pretended not to notice them go.

On one such trip Ewanah brought Swift Arrow good news.

"White Rabbit gave me the information you have long wanted. I told him I wished to know more about my future husband and the life he lived before joining our village. So he set about helping me. He figured that only the old ones of the village would have the information I requested. Yesterday he sat down among some old warriors who were braiding whips. He pretended he wanted to help them with the whips. Then he mentioned the subject of our marriage."

Ewanah evidently enjoyed telling her story, but George felt impatient.

"Well, what did he learn, Ewanah? Tell me quickly!"

Ewanah smiled unperturbed. "Do not be in such a hurry. You must learn patience. Well, when White Rabbit mentioned our marriage, one old brave puffed out his chest and said, 'Ha! I am one of those who found Swift Arrow when he was but a paleface papoose.' Then the old man told him all about the raid on your settlement and how Big Wolf had ordered that a son be found for him. He said that your mother and father were not killed. Your home was not even burned down. They were in a hurry to get away with you two boys; so they had to satisfy themselves with just stealing some things from the house, such as dishes and blankets."

George threw his arms around his sister with joy. "Oh, Ewanah, never have I heard such good news. Ma and Pa are still alive! But which way—what direction does my home lie? How do I get there?"

"White Rabbit found that information for me also. You must go toward the southeast to a place the paleface call Pennsylvania. You will walk two moons and cross many rivers before getting there. Then there is a river, a very wide river, to cross. Your valley lies just beyond the great river."

"Did White Rabbit know the name of the river?"

"Yes, but I do not remember. Oh, what does it matter? The paleface call it by an Indian name, but I do not remember."

Memory came to George's rescue. He knew that White Rabbit had found out the truth, for he remembered now that his homeland had been called Pennsylvania. And he remembered that river too. It had another river which branched off from it. But what was the name of it? So many years had passed since he had thought with English words and names that he could remember them only with great difficulty.

"It is called Sus—Sus—Oh, well, like you say, Ewanah, what does it matter."

"Why, that's it, Swift Arrow! That's what White Rabbit said. Susquehanna!"

"You are very wise, Sister, to learn all of this in so clever a manner. Now I can leave here shortly."

"Oh, Swift Arrow, I do not want you to go," Ewanah cried.

"Do not feel bad, Little Sister. We must each continue in our own way of life. And when I go, you will be able to marry White Rabbit. I am certain Big Wolf will choose him as your husband and as village chief. Big Wolf speaks more highly of him than any other of our braves."

"Swift Arrow," Ewanah said, "are you still praying to your Great

Spirit?"

"Yes. I talk to Him all the time. I am sure He will lead me.

When George returned to the village, he found Big Wolf waiting in an angry mood. "Where have you been? I have need of you. News came today that the paleface are moving more and more into our hunting grounds. Soon they will be trying to build their houses in our own village. They must be stopped. The time will soon come when you must lead our people to war. You will use the torch, the arrow, the tomahawk, and even the paleface's own gun. That is the only language they understand."

Then Big Wolf must have sensed George's dismay. For he hastened to reassure him.

"You are a brave Indian now, my son. You must forget that you ever lived among the paleface. They are not worthy of one so strong and courageous as you."

The horrible scene of the last day at his father's home now passed before George's eyes. He remembered the Indians streaming out the doors with blankets and precious dishes. He remembered Robert's terrified screams. Yet despite the memories, he merely nodded his head in submission to the chief. Not by a flicker of his eyelashes did he reveal his true feelings.

George awoke next morning to find Big Wolf greatly disturbed again, but this time over a completely different matter. It seemed that those in charge of providing food for the wedding feast had overlooked getting a sufficient supply of firewater for all the guests who would be coming from surrounding tribes. Indeed, some of the braves had even drunk up part of the supply that had been on hand in the village. Big Wolf seemed at a loss as to what to do. The wedding would take place in just two days. And what was a wedding feast without firewater?

George's quick mind seized on this problem as an opportunity to help him escape. He just hoped it would work.

"Honored Father," he said, "the place where our firewater is made lies only half a day's journey from here. Why not send braves to get some? They could be back in our village by tomorrow morning."

"You think I would trust those braves with so much firewater? The coming feast and celebration has put them in such an excited mood that along the way they would no doubt drink half of what they brought." This is what George had hoped Big Wolf would say.

"Then there is no answer but that you go with them to make sure nobody touches the firewater," George said. "You have felt so much better the past few weeks that you will enjoy the trip, and the exercise will do your body good."

Big Wolf considered for a few moments.

"Yes, I believe you have the right idea," he said. "I will go. Gather thirty of our most faithful braves, and choose fifty of our strongest horses. It will take at least that many horses to carry the firewater we need."

George did as the chief commanded him. Within an hour the horses were ready, and the men were eager to leave. Before Big Wolf mounted his horse he called to George.

"Swift Arrow, I leave you in full charge of this village while I am gone," Big Wolf said in a voice loud enough to be heard by the people who had gathered to say good-bye. "In case an emergency comes, you will use your wisdom in council with the elders to make a decision."

Then Big Wolf placed his hand on George's big shoulder, and lowering his voice said, "I will see you tomorrow, my son. And then we will have more than enough firewater for your wedding."

George tried to smile but had difficulty. "No, my father," he thought, "you will not see me tomorrow. And the firewater shall not be for my wedding but for the wedding of my good friend, White Rabbit. It is he who will marry Ewanah."

Watching the chief ride off in the morning sunlight, George felt sad. He had endured Big Wolf's stern punishments, but he had also enjoyed his many kindnesses. As the years passed, George had grown to love the man.

"But now I must leave," he thought. "It will be best for all. I could not make a good leader for these people, for I would never lead them to battle when they thought it necessary. I would never stand by and let them hurt one single hair from the head of my people."

George ran to Ewanah's wigwam. "Ewanah! Ewanah!" he called.

The old squaw stuck her head through the wigwam opening and pretended to be angry when she saw it was George.

"Go away, young chief," she said. "You are not to see your bride when the wedding time is so close."

George sighed. "Do not be foolish, old one. I have grown up with her and I will see her if I want to. Now tell her to come to me."

The squaw's head disappeared back inside the wigwam, and Ewanah emerged a short time later. She looked worried.

"The time draws near, Swift Arrow. What do we do?"

"Shh! Do not speak so loudly, my sister. Today is the day I leave. I have a plan, and when I am ready I will let you know. Then we will go for a ride together. Bring a supply of jerked venison with you. Stay close to your wigwam so I can reach you easily."

George walked toward the shelter where he knew he could find what remained of the village's supply of firewater. Along the way he told several men to follow him.

"Help me take this firewater to the arena," he told them. Then pointing to one warrior, he said, "And you, call the braves together and direct them to meet at the arena."

When George and his helpers reached the arena with the casks full

116

of liquor, the other braves were already waiting.

"My friends," George said, "you have worked hard preparing for my wedding feast. A little fun will do you good. Since a new supply of firewater arrives tomorrow, shall we not finish off what we have here?"

The men cheered their agreement and fell to drinking with a will. Before long they were drunkenly approving the new chief. George returned to the arena an hour later and found the casks empty and several braves scattered on the ground sleeping. In the village he found more braves dozing in the sunshine by their wigwams. A few who had not yet had their fill, laughed foolishly as he walked by.

"Now is the time," George thought. "The braves are too drunk to know what I do, and the squaws are not wise enough to care. It will be evening before they know I am missing, and even then most will probably be too sick from the firewater to chase after me."

He hurried to his wigwam and gathered some things he would need. A light blanket, a small flask to hold water, and his bow and arrows.

"When I am unlucky with my bow, I will eat the venison that Ewanah brings, or plants and berries from the forest."

He found Ewanah waiting beside her wigwam, and she followed him to the horse corral without a word.

Reaching the corral, George had an afterthought. "Perhaps you had better not go any farther, Ewanah. The people will want to know why you did not stop me."

"Then you are really leaving now? I am sad. No, I will go with you as far as I dare, just as though we were taking one of our usual rides. I will tell the people that I stopped to rest or watch some animals play. When I returned to the path you were gone."

After riding for about three hours, George told Ewanah to return.

"Now you must go back, Little Sister, so darkness does not catch you in the forest. I could not go in peace if I had to fear for your safety."

Ewanah turned toward him and he saw her eyes filled with tears. He had never seen her look more beautiful.

"Do not cry, Ewanah. I will find happiness among my people, and you will be happy with White Rabbit."

When Ewanah did not move or say anything, George felt like weeping too. How could he leave this lovely creature who had for so long been both a friend and a sister?

"My heart will be with you and your father always, Sister. But go now. You must return."

Ewanah seemed unable to speak, but she touched her hands to her lips and reached it to his cheek. Then she turned and slowly rode back down the trail, her head bent in sorrow.

Now George jumped from Neko, and turned the little pony loose with a slap on the rump.

"Good-bye. You have been a good, faithful friend," he said.

George knew that the pony would find its way back to the village. He could not use it anymore, for now he must leave the trails and travel through the bushes and trees. If he should stay on the trail, his tracks would be easy to follow. He watched Neko and Ewanah until they disappeared; then he plunged into the thick undergrowth.

George swung from the top of a tree on the island to a treetop on the shore. Then he continued swinging through the tall trees.

Chapter 14

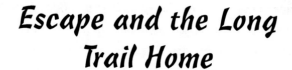

Escape and the Long Trail Home

All the first day after leaving Ewanah and Neko, George traveled through the bushes and around trees. The Indians had taught him how to walk silently and cover the trail, and George had learned his lessons well. Now the Indians' training proved more valuable to him than they had ever guessed it would. He must leave no trail that even Indians could follow. He came across many birds and small animals he could have killed for food with his bow and arrows, but he knew that kindling a cook fire would be too dangerous. If the Indians should be following him, the fire could be seen a long way. So George contented himself with a piece of the venison, some dried corn that Ewanah had also given him, and some sweet huckleberries he found growing wild. At last he crawled into a thicket to sleep for the night.

As the first rays of sunlight began tinting the sky, George was again on his journey. When he first awoke, he noticed how close the trees grew in this part of the forest, and decided to try swinging from tree to tree. "Not even the cleverest Indians could follow my trail in the treetops," he thought.

By nighttime his whole body ached from weariness, and he slept on an island in a small lake. George's muscles still ached when he started next morning, so he decided to walk rather than swing through the treetops. As he traveled he thought of many things.

What about Ma and Pa? Had White Rabbit's information been correct? Were they really alive? He tried to remember the cabin he had helped Pa build. There had been a smooth wooden table and that big fireplace. They ate from dishes and with spoons and forks. For special occasions Ma even had some nice china dishes. He tried to do his thinking in English but had a hard time. The English words were slow in coming. He had spoken nothing but an Indian language for twelve years.

And what about the Indians? Had the braves started after him yet? What had Big Wolf done when he discovered his son was gone? Why, today was even the day that had been set for his wedding! Would Big Wolf let White Rabbit substitute for him?

By noon George found a thicket to hide in for rest. He picked some berries that grew nearby and some plants that he had eaten many times while hunting with the Indians. Then, looking back the way he had come, he saw a moving form in the distance. Yes, the Indians were after him and not far behind!

Without hesitation George ran to a stream that he had been following and dived in, swimming to an island near the opposite shore. A grove of large trees grew on the island. And the channel between the island and other bank was so narrow that George crossed it simply by swinging from the top of a tree on the island to a treetop on shore. Though he still ached from his treetop swinging of the day before, he again took to the trees. As long as he stayed in them he would leave no trail. After about three hours of swinging from tree to tree, George decided he must have lost his followers. And his arms ached so badly he knew he could not go much farther. He jumped to the ground beside a long, fat log. Closer inspection showed that it was hollow, so he decided to crawl inside for some rest. In a few minutes he fell asleep.

Something strange awoke George, and his heart seemed to freeze within him. He was hearing Indian voices! Then he recognized the voice of Sick Dog, one of Big Wolf's bravest warriors. George realized that Sick Dog and at least one other companion were sitting on the very log that he had hidden in!

"I suppose we might as well give up," Sick Dog was saying. "We have seen no trace of him for hours and hours, and when we did it was for only a short distance. Either he is moving in another direction or he has taken to the trees."

"But what is Big Wolf going to say when we tell him we have failed? You know how angry he was when he discovered that Swift Arrow had left."

"Yes. I have never seen him more angry. But we have done our best. Perhaps we could tell him the Potawatomi are on the warpath and stole him. Better that Big Wolf's anger be turned against another tribe than against his own."

Then George heard nothing for a long time and finally heard the men splashing in the river. He climbed out of the log and pushed through some thick undergrowth and scurried quickly across an open grassy field, keeping his body bent low. That night his stomach ached and rumbled for hunger, so he set a rabbit snare. He had long since left his bow and arrows in a treetop because they hindered his swinging. Then he built a small fire and feasted that night on roasted rabbit.

As George continued to travel, he lost track of the days. Some days when he snared a rabbit or partridge, he ate well. Other days he lived on roots, plants, and berries. He knew he had lost some weight, but he still had his strength and courage. He crossed mountains and valleys, swam rivers, and waded through streams; but try as he might he could never recognize the countryside—not until one day when he reached a clearing in the woods that showed signs of many Indian camps having been made there in previous years. A few battered remains of wigwams even lay on the ground. George immediately recognized this place as the campsite where he had stayed so long with old Woonsak. And this was the place where he and Robert had been separated. When he remembered Robert's terrified screams, he could feel no regret for leaving the Indians. Now he only felt anxiety for his real parents. Would he reach the settlement only to find them dead or gone? Maybe the settlement wouldn't even be there any longer. Indians could have destroyed it during the twelve years he had been away.

George traveled another three weeks, here and there recognizing campsites or groves of trees. Then the day came when he arrived on the west bank of the Susquehanna. He looked for a place where the current did not seem too strong, and swam across. Now he knew he had almost come to the end of his journey, and he felt so eager to finish that he scarcely took time to sleep nights.

The leaves of the trees had already begun turning their fall colors when George finally stood at the top of the hill overlooking his valley. He knew this was his valley. The same hills that he remembered well surrounded it, the same streams watered it, and far below he could see a bustling little town. Yes, it looked far too large to call a settlement anymore. Houses dotted the hills, and he saw narrow strips that he knew must be new roads. He could even make out men and women going about their early morning duties. Beyond the homes, the fields of grain were yellow next to green fields of vegetables. He spotted orange pumpkins growing in the fields of ripening corn. He knew men would take up their tools within an hour or two and set about finishing the harvest.

Before moving down the hill, George took time to breathe a simple prayer. "Thank You, God, for bringing me home. I knew You would. Thank You for keeping me safe all these years. And now please help me to find Ma and Pa."

George started along the path, watching smoke plume from the chimneys. Women would be cooking breakfast now over open fires in the big fireplaces. Eggs, pancakes, and por—por—What was that word?—Porridge! Yes, Ma made porridge almost every morning. He came to a road that had been just a path when he lived there. It led him past several houses. Who lived here and across the road and over there? He could not remember. Maybe these houses had been built since he had left. Now he was passing a house he recognized! He and Robert had helped stuff mud into the chinks. He came to another house he recognized. These people had a boy just his age. They called him Ben. George could see men going to barns and small boys carrying pails of frothy milk. A few stared at him curiously, and George realized how odd he must look to them. His clothes were torn and dirty, and his skin was so brown with stain. Yes, his skin! He had forgotten about the stain on his skin and hair. People wouldn't recognize him for sure.

Pa's house must be straight ahead. He remembered that Pa had built it at the head of the valley on a sloping hillside. There it was! And there was the hill near the spring where he and Robert had been captured and dragged away. But the thick trees and bushes that had grown on that hillside had been mostly cut down. Just a few remained for shade, and it looked as if Pa had even planted some of it in corn. But what if Pa didn't still live here?

A man was driving a cow toward George. He would ask him about Pa. George tried to gather the English words he needed but couldn't even move his lips. So much time had passed since he had talked to anybody even in the Indian language that his lips felt stiff. Now the man was staring at him, passing him. He must make himself say something! George cleared his throat.

"Uh, where is the cabin of Marcus Boylan?" he heard himself ask.

His voice sounded high and strained, but at least the words had come easier than he expected.

The man pointed toward the house that George had been watching. Just as he thought! This was the cabin he had lived in, and Pa did still live there. Now he ran toward the cabin. Coming closer, he realized that the cabin had been enlarged. He guessed that at least two more rooms had been added on. And a neat rail fence separated the property from the road. Then George saw a man leave the back door and come around the house with a milk pail in his hand. He headed toward a barn across the road, and he was coming straight toward George! The young man's heart felt full to bursting. This was Pa! This was Marcus Boylan. His thick beard was streaked with silver and so was his curly brown hair. Now his blue eyes surveyed George. They flashed with anger, and he raised his fist.

"Get out of here, you Indian dog. I won't have you lurking about my place."

This so surprised George that he scarcely knew what to do. Then he almost laughed, realizing that of course his father could not recognize him—not with all the brown stain clinging to his skin and hair and with the Indian clothes he was wearing. Why, he even moved like an Indian. The last time Pa had seen him he had been a small lightheaded boy.

At last George gathered his wits and tried to speak. But the English words didn't want to come.

"Me—no—I am no Indian dog—" he stammered, trying to remember what he wanted to say.

Marcus's voice again rose in anger. "Get out of here, I say! I have no work or food for you nor any of you thieving Indians. Sure, I used to be good to you. Always gave you food. But how did you repay me? By stealing my boy, that's how!"

"But, Pa. Pa, it's me!" George cried.

Marcus searched the young man's face. "You're an Indian!"

"No, I am the papoose—the boy—George Boylan. George Augustus Boylan."

Now confusion showed on Marcus's face. How could this Indian know his son's name?

"You can't be!" Marcus shouted. "This is another Indian trick. My son did not have your kind of skin or hair. He had light hair. You are an Indian. Now, get out of here!"

Just then a pretty, white-haired woman appeared behind Marcus. George recognized her right away as Ma. Only now she had little lines of worry drawn tightly across her face.

"Now, Marcus, stop your shouting," Prudence said. "This boy may very well be a fine Indian. I keep telling you that not all Indians are bad."

"But, Prudence, this rascal claims he's our George! Can you beat that? Our George!"

"Ma, please tell him, Ma," George said. "I am George. This is just a stain from berries on my skin."

Now the color drained from Prudence's face. "Of course, Marcus, he would be changed, you know. We remember him as a child, but it has been twelve years. I know! The birthmark on his back and the scar on his head. They could not be changed."

George immediately bent his head low and parted his hair, revealing a long, jagged scar. Then he turned his back and lifted the buckskin shirt. In the middle of his back Prudence could see a dark brown birthmark as large as a shilling.

He turned around and started to speak, but the words were cut off by his mother's loud cry: "George! My boy! You have come back!"

She threw her arms around George. But the shock proved to be too much for her, and she fell back in a faint. George caught her in his strong arms and carried her to the house. Marcus followed and showed him to the new bedroom, where George laid his mother on a soft featherbed. Tears stood in Marcus's eyes, and seeing them, George let the tears fall from his eyes too.

Within just a few minutes Prudence had regained some calmness. Marcus called in neighbors who had known George when he was a child. Then after about an hour of asking him questions about his many experiences, Prudence suddenly began to laugh.

"Land sakes! All us sitting here making him answer so many questions when anybody can tell by looking that he's almost starved to death. What can I fix you to eat, Son?"

In the excitement, George had forgotten all about being hungry. But now he smiled gratefully at his mother.

"Well, eggs, flapjacks, bread, butter, milk, and—and—some porridge!"

Prudence fixed breakfast for the whole happy crowd that had gathered in her front room, and it was several hours before the last of the guests had left. The only sad note of the morning had been when Mrs. Stewart asked about Robert. George had to tell her that the boy had been taken away from him long ago and he had not seen Robert since. But Robert had been gone for so many years that even Mrs. Stewart had lost hope of his returning, so the news had not been so upsetting as it might have been.

Before too long the stain disappeared from George's skin, and his hair returned to its normal rusty blond color. The Boylan cabin rang with laughter and happy voices. It seemed almost impossible to them that their family had been brought together. George spent his days helping Marcus and his evenings visiting with friends of the village. And by Thanksgiving he was spending many of those evenings at the

Stewart home, visiting with Robert's sister Becky. She had grown to be a pretty girl with bright, laughing eyes and a friendly smile. Almost before he knew it, George had fallen in love with her. That Christmas, the first one George had celebrated since he was eight years old, he and Becky were married. They needed no firewater to celebrate their happiness, but Prudence did make a huge fruitcake, and Mrs. Stewart prepared a large feast attended by most of the people of the town.

With the help of other townsmen, George built a cabin across the road from Marcus and Prudence. He wanted to be near his parents to try to make up for the many years he had been away. And they managed to find excuses two or three times a day to visit with him and Becky.

When George and Becky had children, some people thought they were the luckiest children in the whole valley, maybe the luckiest in all of Pennsylvania. For George never ran out of Indian tales to tell and stories of his own adventures with Big Wolf, and he never seemed to grow tired of telling them. Adults enjoyed hearing George's stories too, and his home was often filled with people asking him questions about the strange ways of the Indians or advice about getting along with them.

When George's little daughter became old enough, he made her a special playhouse, a real Indian wigwam. He even covered the floor with a soft bear rug and hung smooth animal skins to cover the walls. Then he told her the story of another little girl, a tiny Indian named Ewanah, who had been delighted with a small log cabin he had built for her.

Years later George's daughter told the stories of Swift Arrow to her own children and grandchildren. And her grandchildren repeated the stories to their grandchildren, so that though George, Marcus, Prudence, Big Wolf, Ewanah, and all their friends died long ago, their story still lives on.

We invite you to view the complete
selection of titles we publish at:

www.TEACHServices.com

or write or email us your praises,
reactions, or thoughts about this
or any other book we publish at:

TEACH Services, Inc.
P.O. Box 954
Ringgold, GA 30736

info@TEACHServices.com

CPSIA information can be obtained at www.ICGtesting.com
Printed in the USA
BVOW03s1207240114

342914BV00006B/10/P